Multimedia Activities
for Students

D1711026

Multimedia Activities for Students

A Teachers' and Librarians' Handbook

by Barbara Head Sorrow

McFarland & Company, Inc., Publishers
Jefferson, North Carolina, and London

British Library Cataloguing-in-Publication data are available

Library of Congress Cataloguing-in-Publication Data

Sorrow, Barbara.
    Multimedia activities for students : a teachers' and librarians'
handbook / by Barbara Head Sorrow.
        p.   cm.
    Includes bibliographical references and index.
    ISBN 0-7864-0211-3 (sewn softcover : 50# alkaline paper)
    1. Interactive multimedia — Handbooks, manuals, etc.
    2. Computer-assisted instruction — Handbooks, manuals, etc.
    3. Media programs (Education) — Handbooks, manuals, etc.
    4. Multimedia systems — Handbooks, manuals, etc.
    5. Multimedia systems industry — United States — Directories.
    I. Title.
    LB1028.55.S67   1997
    371.3'34 — dc20   96-43907
                                                                              CIP

Manufactured in the United States of America

McFarland & Company, Inc., Publishers
Box 611, Jefferson, North Carolina 28640

Table of Contents

Preface

Multimedia Activities for Students is a collection of multimedia ideas and activities that have been utilized in classrooms and libraries with success. The multimedia resources are reliable and authoritative and are appropriate for the classroom and library.

The author has focused on methods that use multimedia or combinations of electronic information and are appropriate for students of all ages. The teacher or librarian can adapt any activity to the grade and achievement level of the student. There are a number of student worksheets included in this text for the convenience of the instructor. Although the forms can be used exactly as they appear in this book, it is recommended that the originals be photocopied at 120 percent for optimal student use.

Emphasis has been placed on the creative learning of the student. The focus is on the programs and resources and not the technology.

Technology

Technology is changing the prevailing vision of learning. Schools are having to educate a new generation of students to compete and cope with technology on a daily basis. As information grows so rapidly in volume, texture, and sophistication, textbooks and traditional classrooms will no longer carry the burden of keeping up with the "information overload." The growth of information mentioned above and the increasing pressure on people's time will demand that teachers and students focus on educational technology to accumulate, store, locate, and manipulate data efficiently. CD-ROM instructional technology is part of the multimedia revolution toward a new classroom environment in which all styles of learning are enhanced.

Multimedia may be defined as the ability to combine and utilize communications media, such as text, graphic art, sound, animation and video for the presentation of information. Multimedia technology focuses on relationships among visual, aural, and textual compositions. Technology which brings together at least two of the following media: text, graphics, video, art, animation and sound, in a single user controlled environment and allows the user to manipulate the elements is called active or interactive multimedia. Active multimedia allows for creative expression while passive multimedia allows only a single path for the user to follow. For example, the user may hear and see John F. Kennedy giving his inaugural speech but not be able to communicate or interact with the media.

Multimedia technology in education offers the learner a unique environment for interactivity, creative expression, student interest and motivation and knowledge mastery. Many multimedia programs which are available are excellent educational tools to enhance the learning process. Some programs are so technical and academic that they could be called multi-sensory text because of the visual, aural, and textual compositions.

Educators need not fear that all multimedia programs are computer games with little value to enhance the curriculum because many programs which are available on CD-ROM have the same basic reference information that can be found in most libraries. The electronic images, animation, graphics, and text have been added to allow the learner an opportunity to learn at a pace which promotes academic achievement and individual learning.

Following are suggestions to help the multimedia process be more effective: (1) To determine goals and objectives consider the curriculum the school supports. (2) Instructional objectives may be broken down to learning tasks. (3) The technical literacy of the students and the profile of the class should be considered. (4) Utilize teaching methods which are compatible with the lesson objective. (5) Select appropriate multimedia. (6) Sequence and scope the student objectives with evaluative criteria. (7) Discuss lesson plans with other team educators.

Multimedia should be an integral part of the student's instructional program. It can be the tool which students can use effectively to gather, record, understand, and utilize information. Because multimedia is so adaptable to the many different learning styles it may be the best tool to concentrate on in the classroom or media center.

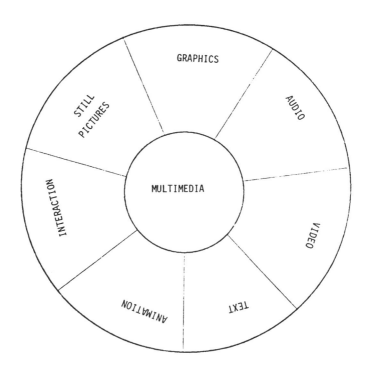

Multimedia is a growing and changing technology. It was at first hampered by a lack of standardization, but a group of companies formed the Multimedia PC Marketing Council and formulated a set of multimedia standards.

In 1990 the original MPC standards and specifications were issued and are now referred to as MPC Level 1. Products that conform to the minimum specifications will display the MPC logo. In 1993 Level 2 MPC specifications were issued by the Multimedia Marketing Council. The following specifications are listed below:

Level I	Level II
HARDWARE	HARDWARE
386SX	486SX, 25MHz
2M Minimum RAM	4M
30M Hard Drive	160M
150K CD-ROM Xfer	300K
1000ms seek	400ms
CD-Audio	CD-Audio,CD-XA
8 bit sound card	8 or 16 bit sound card
11kHz, 22kHz rates	1kHz, 22kHz, 44.1kHz

Many multimedia programs run through Windows and Windows 95 and will need more RAM than the above level 1 and 2 specifications. However, remember this is just a standard to go by, and, before you purchase or upgrade your hardware, check the specifications on multimedia software which you want to use and check those specification requirements against the hardware you are planning to purchase or upgrade. There are many technical books on basic information concerning PC hardware and software standards.

CD-ROM is part of this exciting technology, which allows for the instant processing of information, enhancing all styles of learning. Some of the specific learning styles which students are bringing to the classroom are visual, informal, manipulative, dyadic, mobile, haptic, and auditory. According to EBSCO Publishing, CD-ROM has actually grown out of the successful audio CD business. On a CD-ROM disc, over 700 million characters of data can be stored — that's the equivalent of nearly 2,000 floppy disks or of the text in six sets of encyclopedias. The tremendous amount of information that can be stored on such a small surface makes CD-ROM a very appealing technology.

CD-ROM DATABASE
DATA STATION ACTIVITY SHEET

CD-ROM is a new storage medium on a laser disk that can serve as a quick, economical source of information for students, researchers, writers, and professionals across the curriculum. *Grolier Encyclopedia* is one of the most popular products on CD-ROM, which is found in the reference area.

Humanities Index, Readers' Guide to Periodical Literature, Business Periodicals Index, Applied Science and Technology Index, and *ERIC* are a few of the available databases that will aid the research student.

DIRECTIONS

1. Visit the CD-ROM station and become acquainted with the available databases. Check the databases that are available at this station.
    _____ *Applied Science & Technology*
    _____ *Grolier Encyclopedia*
    _____ *PC Globe*
    _____ *World Almanac*
    _____ *Bartlett's Familiar Quotations*
    _____ *Readers' Guide to Periodical Literature*

2. Choose a database that interests you and tell how you could use this information. _____
    _____
    _____
    _____

3. Did you get help from a library staff member?
    Yes_____ No_____

4. Find an article or information pertinent to the year 2000. Summarize the article. _____
    _____
    _____
    _____

STUDENT CRITERIA FOR ANALYZING
ELECTRONIC INFORMATION

The student or groups of students will use this evaluation tool as they research their topics using web sites, CD-ROMS, videos, lasers, and video conferencing.

		YES	NO
ACCURACY	Is the information factual?		
APPROPRIATENESS	Is the information appropriate for the subject and age group?		
AUTHORITATIVE	Are the authors qualified to write on this subject?		
CONTENT	What is the value of the material? Does it contribute to the subject?		
DOCUMENTATION	Does the information explain the source or author?		
EASE OF USE	Is the information easy to search and easy to print or manipulate?		
ILLUSTRATIONS	Do the illustrations coincide with the text?		
INDEX	Is the information indexed? Do the search engines retrieve sufficiently?		
RELIABILITY	Can the user depend upon the information being accurate and available in other authoritative sources?		
BIBLIOGRAPHY	Are there accurate and reliable citations provided for the information?		

There are many informative sources on how to make multimedia presentations for the educational community. Tay Vaughan's *Multimedia: Making It Work* is an excellent book on the basics of multimedia presentations. Sorel Reisman has an excellent book also, *Multimedia Computing: Preparing for the 21st Century*. These books go into the step-by-step directions and concepts of multimedia. The information presented in this book focuses on activities and ideas for the classroom and media center and gives an overview of the technical aspects of multimedia.

Hypertext and hypermedia are terms and concepts which educators and students will understand as they search data and create a multimedia presentation.

Hypertext may be explained as information organized into a set of nodes and connected by links so that the information can be accessed non-sequentially. For example, links connect Abraham Lincoln with the nickname "Abe." Text segments, or nodes, are accessed by links which act as keywords or main terms. In a fully indexed system, like *INFOTRAC* or *Wilson's Electronic Readers' Guide to Periodical Literature*, words or subjects can be accessed immediately by hypertext. If you entered the main term "lasers," the following information may be brought to the screen with the correct number of entries for each one.

LASERS	25 entries
LASER/HISTORY	10 entries
LASER/PATENTS	5 entries
LASER/WEAPONS	16 entries
LASER/SURGERY	23 entries

Hypertext also links associated images, graphics, sounds and video clips. When this interaction and linking occurs with multimedia, multimedia may become hypermedia if the navigation system is nonlinear.

Multimedia presentations are important methods for educators to use to present classroom instruction because they can create presentations to fit the classroom profile and to meet students' individual needs. Students can also create their own presentations through multimedia which provides a means to express their personality and individualistic styles. For example, students who are artistic can focus on graphics, while those students who enjoy music may express their feelings with sound. A class may have another Charles Schulz or Walt Disney and these students would have the opportunity to utilize animation in their presentations.

The following software presentation tools have had good reviews in computer magazines and by professional presenters:

Program	Publisher
Harvard Graphics	Software Publishing
Hollywood	Claris Corp.
Persuasion	Aldus Corp.
Powerpoint	Microsoft Corp.
Softcraft Presenter	Softcraft Corp.
Stanford Graphics	3 Divisions Corp.
Wordperfect	Wordperfect Corp.
Tempra Media Author	Mathematica Corp.
Compel	Asymetrix Corp.

Before you purchase a program, goals and objectives need to be written by a multimedia team of educators and students. Planning for multimedia is a very important stage when utilizing multimedia. Stages of the multimedia presentation process are presented in below.

STAGE I	Planning
STAGE II	Defining
STAGE III	Production
STAGE IV	Evaluation

The first stage is planning which involves goals and objectives, lesson/curriculum, grade/audience, information/content, and evaluation. The next stage is defining the elements in the planning stage. For example, the teaching team needs to define the curriculum goals and objectives and the skills which need to be mastered by the students.

The technical literacy of the audience needs to be identified next before the class decides what type of presentation and the time frame. The abilities and educational achievement of the audience, ages, background, grade level and communication skills need to be considered. Who will see the production? What are the expectations and needs of the audience? Also, what types of media will be combined in the multimedia presentation to convey the objective of the presentation? These questions will help make the presentation more meaningful. The content of the presentation and appropriate media which will be used is a primary consideration. The combination of graphics and animation with sound may be better than text and music. These decisions have to be made by the multimedia team.

The production process of the multimedia presentation begins with gathering and organizing the information. Deciding on the words or text which should be emphasized and the format which will be used with the combination of audio, video, graphics, still pictures, music, animation and interaction is a complex consideration of the process. Media production is a cooperative learning endeavor.

The evaluation process is very important because this is where the students and teachers have to make decisions about the quality of the instruction or presentation. Decisions have to be made to leave certain elements out or add specific information and combinations of media to make the presentation more effective. When evaluating the presentation, consider the technical quality as well as the instructional design of the product. Refer back to the goals and objectives and evaluate the outcomes defined by the instructional tasks and objectives.

The following exercises give the student the experience of producing a slide presentation. This exercise uses the program *PowerPoint* but can be adapted to other similar programs. Each exercise builds on the skill and knowledge of the earlier tasks. As the user develops expertise in producing a presentation it would be wise if the student would select a "how to book" on multimedia presentations so video, audio, and animation could be added to text and graphics to create a professional presentation. More and more students are being required to present their research in a multimedia-type presentation as compared to the standard research paper.

Presentation: Exercise 1

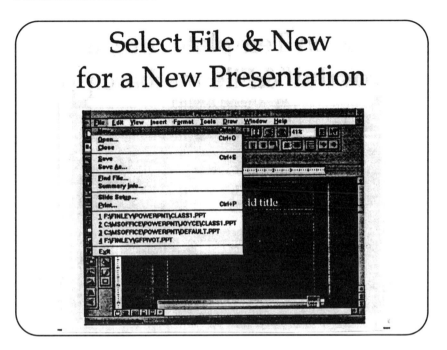

1. Open PowerPoint and select "New Presentation."
2. Select **Blank Presentation**.
3. Select the first choice in the "Auto Layout" screen.
4. Single click in the Title area of the screen and type:
      THE TITLE OF THE PRESENTATION
5. Single click in the subtitle area of the screen and type:
      TOPICS AND AUTHORS OF PRESENTATION

Presentation: Exercise 2

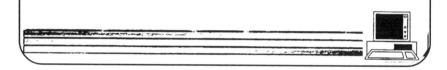

MULTIMEDIA
PRESENTATION

SLIDES, OUTLINE, SPEAKER
NOTES, AUDIENCE HANDOUTS

1. Click the NEW SLIDE button at the bottom of the screen.
2. Click in the Title area and type:
         MULTIMEDIA PRESENTATION
3. Click in the subtitle area of the screen and type:
         SLIDES, OUTLINE, SPEAKER NOTES,
               AUDIENCE HANDOUTS
4. Click New Slide.

Presentation: Exercise 3

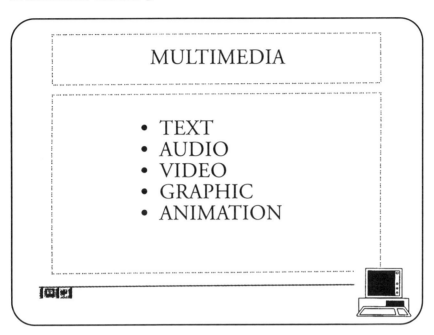

1. Create a new slide by selecting the second layout on the Auto Layout screen.
2. In the title area, type:
   MULTIMEDIA
3. In the body area, position the cursor in the first column and click. Click on the right mouse button; select **Bullet...**, then click in the box entitled "Use a bullet."
4. Type the following:
   - TEXT
   - AUDIO
   - VIDEO
   - GRAPHIC
   - ANIMATION
5. Click New Slide.

Presentation: Exercise 4

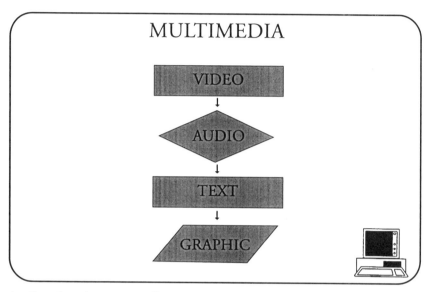

1. On the *drawing toolbar* on the left of the screen, click on the **autoshapes** button.
2. Select the **rectangle** button and draw a rectangle.
3. With the rectangle selected, type:
   VIDEO
   Drag one of the handles on a perpendicular side to resize the rectangle.
4. Click on the **diamond** button and draw a diamond.
5. With the diamond selected, type:
   AUDIO
6. Resize the diamond and move it under the rectangle.
7. Click the rectangle, move it under the diamond, highlight the text and type:
   TEXT
8. Select the **parallelogram** button and draw a parallelogram. Type:
   GRAPHIC
9. Using the **line** on the toolbar, connect the shapes as shown.

Presentation: Exercise 5

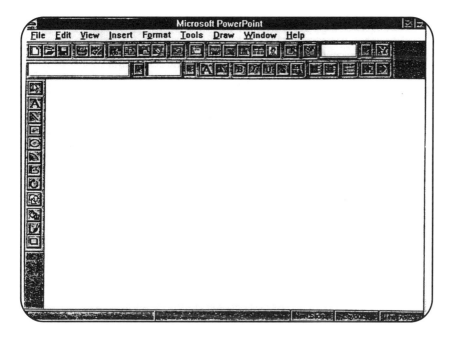

Getting Help

1. Open PowerPoint.
2. Close the dialog boxes.
3. Move the mouse pointer to one of the tools. The name of the tool is displayed.
4. Look at the Status Bar. A description of the tool is displayed.
5. Click the Help Tool.
6. Click the Contents button to see the Help contents.
7. Click Overview of PowerPoint.
8. Continue getting help by double-clicking Online Help.

Presentation: Exercise 6

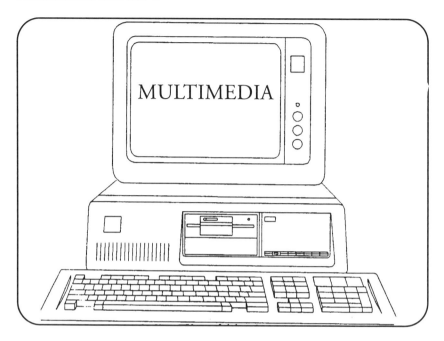

Clip Art

1. Go to view. Then select the correct slide.
2. Go to the **Insert Menu** and select **Clip Art**.
3. Scan through the list of categories and select "Technology."
4. Select the PC and click **OK**. This will put a picture of the computer on the slide.
5. Resize the computer to fit the screen/slide.
6. To go back to the multimedia presentation, use the view menu.

Information

Information in the 21st Century

The research process is a logical process by which scattered knowledge is organized, analyzed, and utilized.

The student goes through the same process with electronic information as traditional print sources. The following steps will be discussed.

1. Select the topic
2. Define the topic
3. Ask questions about the topic
4. Select the key words or main terms
5. Gather information about the topic
6. Organize information
7. Analyze information
8. Utilize information

Selecting the subject or topic comes first. The classroom teacher or librarian may suggest a topic or the ideas may come from the subject being studied. The student may have options to research a topic which is of interest to him. Sometimes, it is suggested that the student conduct a library or media survey to see if there is enough information about a topic before a decision is made about the topic selection. This may save time and time is an important factor in the search process.

After the library survey the student may want to define the topic. Often the topic is too broad because it contains too many elements. Japan, for example, would be too broad to search and would need to be defined and narrowed in order to focus and organize the information or data.

Descriptions and definitions make the searching process much easier to organize and focus on the topic. Dates, places, people, events, occupations, and contributions all assist the researcher with defining the topic.

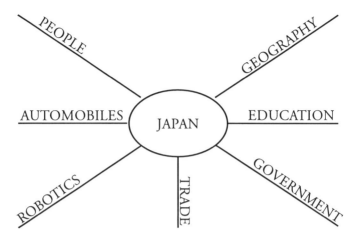

Therefore, these descriptions, which help narrow the topic, will be referred as descriptors of the main terms or key words.

When the student is in the process of an electronic search the data on the computer screen may be divided into descriptors. For example, Japan may be narrowed into sub-headings, such as history, education, environment, etc.

> JAPAN
> Environment
> History
> People

The method of electronic data organization makes searching easier for the student. The student can see the way the data or information is organized and defined. If a student chooses to research the cotton gin, Eli Whitney would certainly help define the topic. The dates and time period would assist the student with an understanding of the importance of this invention. The area or place the invention was used would also contribute to the project. Descriptors will play an important part in the process of gathering, organizing, analyzing, and utilizing information.

Questions

After the topic is defined and narrowed it is time to explore ways of gathering information. One way to formulate the research problem or topic is to put it into interrogative form. For example, a sample question may be: How has education in Japan changed since World War II? Or if that topic is too broad and there are too many changes since World War II the researcher may want to focus on the education process in Japan during the past five years. Answers to these questions will describe the situation. The "why, where, what, when, who" questions will focus on the problem and help to determine how and why conditions have come about. This accomplishes a portion of the purposes of research. Questions will focus the problem and help the student or user gather and organize information that may be relevant to the research problem.

Other questions the students will ask as they continue to search are: what kind of question is needed?, what format of information will be best?, which main terms do I need to search?

A famous person would be an easy practice topic. For an English class, students could find information on famous writers. This allows students to become familiar with writers through research rather than teacher lecture. For science, history, philosophy, or sociology, the student could research a famous person in that area to enhance his knowledge in each specific discipline.

The students should be divided into small groups of three or four persons. The teacher should assign a high-achiever to each group.

The teacher will assign each group a question to research about their person. Each group should try to be as thorough as possible in answering the question and evaluating the factual accuracy of the information that they are researching.

```
┌───────────── SEARCH HEADING ─────────────┐
│      Enter the subject or name you wish to find:      │
│        ┌─────────────────────────┐        │
│        │                         │        │
│        └─────────────────────────┘        │
│            then press Enter to search.            │
└───────────────────────────────────────────┘
```

I have a question.

Information: Exercise 1

DESCRIPTORS

1. Main Terms and Key Words
2. Important Dates
3. Places
4. People
5. Subjects
6. Contribution/Occupation

Main Subject Heading   Subheading

_____   _____

_____   _____

_____   _____

_____   _____

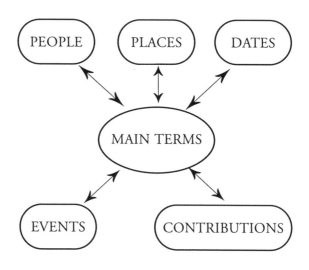

Information: Exercise 2

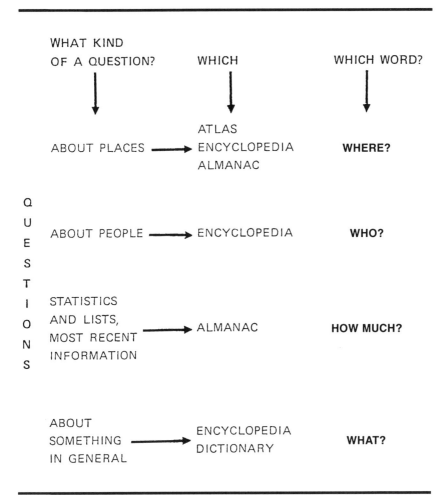

WHAT KIND OF A QUESTION?	WHICH	WHICH WORD?
ABOUT PLACES ⟶	ATLAS ENCYCLOPEDIA ALMANAC	**WHERE?**
ABOUT PEOPLE ⟶	ENCYCLOPEDIA	**WHO?**
STATISTICS AND LISTS, MOST RECENT INFORMATION ⟶	ALMANAC	**HOW MUCH?**
ABOUT SOMETHING IN GENERAL ⟶	ENCYCLOPEDIA DICTIONARY	**WHAT?**

QUESTIONS

Are you searching for?

Background or Biographical Information → Encyclopedia

Facts, Definitions, Brief Information → Dictionary, Handbook, Atlas

Books, Resources → Card Catalog, Online Catalog

Up-to-date Information → Periodical Indexes, CD-ROM-Database

Information: Exercise 3

The use of data requires appropriate questions for an effective multimedia data search. Some questions which you might ask at the beginning of the search process are:

- Why does this topic interest me?
- If I choose this topic, will I be able to gather relevant information?
- Will I be able to find enough appropriate sources from electronic CD-ROM sources or online sources?
- Do I have enough time?
- Have I started questions with what, who, when, where, why, how, should, could, would, and are?
- Do I have enough questions to get an idea about the topic?
- Do my questions match my topic?

Questions: _____

_____

_____

_____

_____

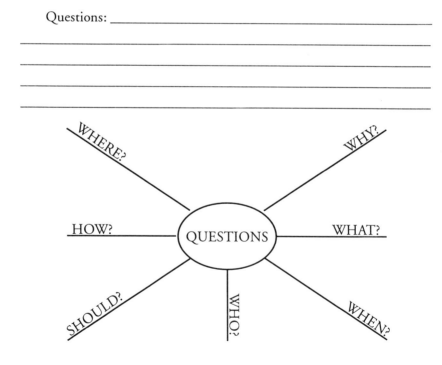

STUDENT WORK SHEET

Name _____

Class _____

Topic _____

Questions:

What do I want to know about this topic? _____

_____

What questions can be asked about my topic? _____

_____

Have I started questions with **What, Who, When, Where, Why, How, Should, Could, Would,** and **Are?** _____

Have I used important verbs such as **compare, define, describe, explain, identify, name,** and **predict** in my questions? _____

Questions:

1. _____

_____

2. _____

_____

3. _____

_____

Now that students have had an introduction to the search process, it is time for them to select a topic. Begin by asking students to make a list of topics that they are interested in learning more about. Why does this topic or subject interest them? Is there sufficient information or data about this topic to conduct a search and be able to produce or utilize the information for a product or presentation. The students may want to list several topics and then conduct a media survey to see which topic would be best for them and the class requirements. Students must select topics which they are personally interested in learning more about. They must be qualified by age and experience to handle and deal with the time limitations. Also, for students to be able to be creative thinkers, they need to choose a topic which leads to investigative and strategic searching.

Another important consideration about the search process is the media format or data which the students need to produce a final product. Does the student need Dr. Martin Luther King's "I Have a Dream" speech in full text, video, audio, or laser disc to produce the documentary at the conclusion of the search? Or does the teacher need a multimedia simulated tutorial for the student to practice basic phonetic skills? Could the music teacher use a multimedia presentation to teach a class on music appreciation and the art teacher a multimedia program to bring the great art masters into the classroom? Multimedia (online and database) can bring graphics, maps, video, and full text to the user. The user's responsibility is to choose the correct type of data and organize it into a method of utilization for the user, student, teacher, classroom, or society.

Collecting and Gathering Information

The users may begin the process of collecting information by familiarizing themselves with the available resources. The online catalog, which is a general listing of the resources, may be a good place to begin. Most libraries have electronic printouts of the resources so the users can immediately print the bibliographic information. If there is a problem locating the resources, ask a librarian or educator for help. They can save the user much valuable time when collecting data.

Since there may be a considerable amount of print and non-print information on the topic available, perseverance is very important for a successful search. The electronic encyclopedia may be a good place to get general and background information. This information will also give the

Information: Exercise 4

INFORMATION SURVEY

Objective: To get an idea about how much and the type of information that is available on this topic.

State your topic _____

List the main terms and key words _____

_____

List important people having to do with the topic _____

_____

List places _____

_____

List important dates _____

_____

List contributions, inventions, or occupations having to do with the topic

_____

_____

List the title of one multimedia program which could help with the topic

_____

_____

List one citation of a periodical which seems to deal directly with the topic

_____

_____

List other types of information (maps, videos, CD-ROM) which are available for preview _____

_____

_____

_____

---

user clues for additional sources of information. Many libraries or media centers have CD-ROM talking dictionaries in many different languages. This source may help with a definition of the topic.

If the user is searching a current topic which has been in the news, INFOTRAC, published by Information Access, is a periodical index with full text articles from magazines and journals. NEWSBANK, which is a full text newspaper database of newspapers from across the country, is an excellent database because the user can read different viewpoints of controversial information.

The worksheet in Exercise 5 could help the student keep up with the multimedia being evaluated. Web sites are easily forgotten if they are not immediately recorded.

Wilson's Electronic Database

READERS' GUIDE TO PERIODICAL LITERATURE
DATA STATION ACTIVITY SHEET

The *Readers' Guide to Periodical Literature*, a well-known and widely used index, contains a list of periodical articles arranged in alphabetical order by subject and author. The *Readers' Guide* indexes over 180 popular periodicals, or magazines, such as *Newsweek, Cosmopolitan, Sports Illustrated,* and *Psychology Today.* If looking for an article on a topic currently in the news, popular opinion, or the layman's approach to a topic, this index will be most helpful.

Common Abbreviations		*Month Abbreviations*			
il	illustrations	Ja	January	Ju	July
ed	editor, edited, edition	F	February	Ag	August
q	quarterly	Mr	March	S	September
abr	abridged	Ap	April	O	October
bi-w	biweekly	My	May	N	November
cont	continued	Je	June	D	December

Students and teachers may want to practice oral or written exercises on the *Readers' Guide to Periodical Literature* abbreviations. Electronic information will be in the same format for periodical sources as standard print.

Information: Exercise 5

MULTIMEDIA SOURCE LOG

Multimedia title _____ Description _____

Author/Editor_____ _____

Publication Date_____ _____

Multimedia title _____ _____

Author/Editor_____ _____

Publication Date_____ _____

Multimedia title _____ _____

Author/Editor_____ _____

Publication Date_____ _____

Multimedia title _____ _____

Author/Editor_____ _____

Publication Date_____ _____

Notes _____

_____

_____

_____

_____

_____

STUDENT WORKSHEET

Periodical Index

Find an article on your topic: _____

_____

Under what subject heading did you find your article? _____

_____

Name the title of the article: _____

_____

Author of the article: _____

_____

Title of periodical or journal: _____

_____

Date of periodical: _____

Pages where article will be found: _____

Full text or abstract: _____

Search terms used: _____

_____

Do you think the author is qualified to write this article? Is there any available information about the author? _____

_____

_____

Information: Exercise 6

> *Bird of Happiness.* R. Wilder. il *Sci Dig* 91:112+ F '83
> *Science Digest* volume 91 pages 112+ February 1983

DIRECTIONS

Read the example of a citation above and answer the following questions:

1. Write the title of the magazine: _____

_____

2. Write the author of the article: _____

_____

3. Write the name of the article: _____

_____

4. Write the volume number, date, and page number: _____

_____

5. Find a citation in *INFOTRAC* which could help you get information for your future occupation. Write a summary or synopsis of the article.

_____

_____

_____

_____

This exercise will help the student recognize bibliographic information and organize it into the correct form (MLA, APA).

Accessing Multimedia CD-ROM

LESSON PLAN

Goal: To introduce students to electronic research.
    To acquaint students with logical operators and to narrow or broaden a search.
    To teach students to assess and use the results of their search.

Objectives: Students will learn the techniques and methods of searching CD-ROM information.
    Students will learn to search authors, titles, and subjects.
    Students will use search results.

Activities: Teacher will explain the operation of electronic research.
    Teacher will explain the menu and the options available at the work stations.

The most difficult part of conducting a successful search is selecting the correct term or terms and knowing how to combine them. This requires the students to think critically about what they want to accomplish from the search. The students may combine terms using what is called Boolean logic which refers back to the set theory. In order to narrow the search the sets can be combined using "and," "or," or "not."

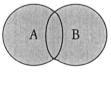

Shaded area shows A OR B. The OR function is used to broaden a search. It retrieves records that contain terms A or B or both A and B.

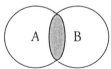

Shaded area shows A AND B. The AND function is used to narrow a search. It retrieves records that contain both A and B.

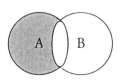

Shaded area shows A NOT B. The NOT function is used to narrow a search. It retrieves records that contain term A and eliminates those that contain term B.

Multimedia Reference Guide

Read and become familiar with the directions of each multimedia program.

Look at the top of the computer screen.

Check to see if the correct CD-ROM is in the computer.

Type in your main term or terms.

Press Enter to see entries for highlighting subjects.

Put the cursor on the line you wish to search.

Press the Enter key.

Check to see if the information is in the correct media form. (Video, maps, full text, periodical citation, music.)

Example: Word search
Browse article titles
Knowledge tree
Timeline
Multimedia

Basic commands: F1 to "help"
F2 to "find"
F3 to "to change discs"
F4 to "show"
F5 to "view"
F6 to "print"
F7 to "restart"
F8 to "view related terms"
F9 to "view thesaurus"
F10 "command menu"

MULTIMEDIA DAILY LESSON PLAN FORM

Teacher: _____ Date of lesson: _____

Subject: _____ Period: _____Grade:_____

Unit title: _____

Goals: _____

Instructional objectives: _____

_____

Student entry level: _____

Technology literacy level: _____

Set: _____

Teaching methods: _____

Monitoring and evaluation: _____

_____

Supervised practice: _____

_____

Closure: _____

Independent practice: _____

_____

Multimedia resources: _____

Hardware resources: _____

World Wide Web Sites: _____

_____

_____

Research via the Internet   by Steve S. Pec

Internet, with over 100 million available records (the Library of Congress alone has 28 million records [and growing] on the Internet), is a rich source of information. However, accessing it remains a problem for both the knowledgeable user and the general public.

First, research via the Internet takes time. The Internet lacks universal standards. It is an unstructured information resource with no subject organization, no comprehensive index, and no control of quality. Second, the general public assumes wrongly that "point and click" will bring results or that information retrieval will be as straightforward as with electronic sources in the library.

To make research via the Internet manageable and productive, one needs to use the correct Internet search tools. The number of such tools exceeds 100 and is growing. They are difficult to classify but, in general, fall into two broad categories: indexes (also known as catalogs, directories or subject trees) and search engines.

Indexes organize resources by subject. The directory is created by human or by a machine called a robot or spider. The user clicks on a selected broad topic then on further sub-categories until a listing of a site or a document is given. Examples of indexes and search engines are:

Internet Public Library   **URL: http://ipl.sils.umich.edu/**
Reference collection contains links with descriptive annotations to selected sites. It offers an on-duty librarian to answer queries.

Magellan   **URL: http://www.mckinley.com**
A subject arranged directory with a search engine. The only index that gives returns with no adult content to them.

Point Communications   **URL: http://www.pointcom.com**
Offers ten broad subjects with further sub-categories, with reviews of the best Web sites on a scale of one to fifty.

Planet Earth   **URL: http://www.uwm.edu/Mirror/inet.services.html**
The resources are presented graphically as an "image map." This is slow to load, but worthy. It also has search capability.

WWW Virtual Library   **URL: http://www.w3.org/hypertext/ DataSources/bySubject/overview.html**
Considered the best catalog. It comes from Switzerland but it is a cooperative effort of over fifty institutions — many from the U.S. Each institution contributes its own specialized subject index. Switzerland provides a searchable centralized index for all participating institutions.

Yahoo   **URL: http://www.Yahoo.com**
The best known and most popular subject directory. It has its own search engine that does not support Boolean searches, but it has metasearch capability (connects to other search engines).

Search engines rely on a computer to continuously comb the Internet for information. Robots are able to automatically update information and change or eliminate dead links. The user gets a listing of sites more or less relevant to a desired topic. Successful search engines are:

Alta Vista   URL: http://www.altavista.digital.com

Searches over 21 million Web pages and Newsgroups. It allows the use of Boolean operators: AND, OR, NOT and NEAR. Use quotes (" ") to search for a specific phrase/topic. Use the plus (+) sign to assure the presence of a specific word. Use the minus (-) sign to filter out an unwanted word.

Excite   URL: http://www.excite.com/query.html

Searches Web and Newsgroups by keyword or concept. If you like the results, click on a given icon for similar documents. This is Excite's way of refining the search. It also offers a catalog of reviewed sites and the past two weeks of Usenet news.

InfoSeek   URL: http://www2.infoseek.com/Query?

Searches the Web and Newsgroups in two ways: InfoSeek Guide and InfoSeek Professional. The first is free; the second is not. InfoSeek Guide searches by keywords and phrases. Use the plus (+) sign to request the presence of a specific word. Use quotes (" ") to search for a specific phrase/topic. Use a hyphen (-) to indicate terms that must be within one word of each other. InfoSeek Guide includes a selective directory of reviewed Internet sites. The directory includes cross-references and a searchable thesaurus. It is known for its ability to search Usenet extensively.

Lycos   URL: http://lycos.cs.cmu.edu/

Searches 19 million Web pages, gopher and FTP sites. Search results indicate how many terms in the search phrase were matched. By default, it searches for occurrences of any specified word, not all of them together. You can change this by adding the Boolean operator AND. You can also set the minimum number of terms that must be matched.

OpenText   URL: http://www.opentext.com

Searches Web pages, gophers and FTP sites. There are three search options. Simple Search is like any ordinary search engine. Power Search searches by five specific fields (anywhere, summary, title, heading, URL) and Boolean operators (AND, OR, NOT, NEAR, FOLLOWED BY). Weighted Search allows the assignment of relative term weights to the Power Search. The default setting is Simple Search.

Webcrawler   URL: http://webcrawler.com/

Searches Web pages, gophers and FTP sites by keywords only. The default is with a Boolean AND. It can be switched off by using the OR operator. The search accepts truncation and is simple and quick. The results are not as extensive as Alta Vista or Lycos.

In using the above mentioned search tools, you will notice that search results vary from one to another. The reasons are too many to mention here. The upshot is that you will need to use a variety of different search tools in order to have some success in doing research via the Internet. If you find the above confusing, consult the "help file" that each search tool has.

Cooperative Learning with Multimedia

Cooperative learning with multimedia is an excellent educational strategy to instruct students with problem solving techniques and skills. Providing students with opportunities to do productive work is the main element in cooperative learning which is built around the school or class curriculum. The central characteristic of cooperative learning is the provision of work opportunities which are intended to be learning experiences.

The class will need to understand the guidelines and directions for a cooperative learning project. The teacher may want to divide the students by grade level, heterogeneous grouping, technical literacy and ability and other educational and personality factors which would have an impact on the group working successfully together.

Each group should be given a specific area of the room to work and plan for maximum comfort. The class as a whole should be given general directions on how to function as a cooperative learning group. Usually, the students will choose a different leader each day until each member of the group has had an opportunity to be a leader. Of course, it is the leader's responsibility to keep the group on task and promote learning.

It is interesting to study students working cooperatively in groups with multimedia because there forms a bond between students when they are working together with electronic information and computer technology. They will help each other and continue to bond within the group even though their friends may or may not be within the group. They seem to pool their strengths and weaknesses to come up with a solution to their specific problem. For example, students who may be studying a unit on Japan may be divided into groups to work on the cultural aspects of the country. One group may work with the cultural history of the past. Group

II may work on music. Group III may work on art. Group IV may work on dance. Group V may work on literature. Within each subject the group will have to divide this topic further into subtopics. Music could be divided into classical, rock, etc. This division would probably depend on what is found in the search process.

The teacher will have to decide on the amount of time to spend researching and analyzing the information found. Then the students will need to prepare their information to be organized in an acceptable matter to present to the class. The group will decide on the spokesperson, the time keeper, multimedia presenter and other team members. If the group is using an electronic presentation, such as PowerPoint, this will require more planning within each group. However, if the group is delivering their presentation without technology they may want each person to contribute to the presentation by dividing the information into areas of interest within the group. The main objective with this lesson is to research information from the CD-ROM multimedia programs and analyze and organize this information into an acceptable method of utilization. These cooperative learning skills, technology and informational skills will be in demand in the educational arena and also workplace.

Usually, self-concept and communication skills improve because of the interaction within the class and groups while demonstrating cooperative behavior. The students develop a concern for each other as they learn to depend upon each other. Writing skills usually improve greatly because of peer interaction and teacher and librarian instruction.

As the students plan their project and utilize multimedia searches the following "Cooperative Learning Search Log" will help them evaluate and organize their information.

COOPERATIVE LEARNING SEARCH LOG

Group _____

Date _____

Name _____

Topic _____

Multimedia/Resources Evaluated:

CD-ROM _____

_____

_____

Web Sites _____

_____

Videos _____

Books _____

_____

Periodicals _____

_____

Interviews _____

Other _____

Multimedia/Resources Selected:

CD-ROM _____

Web Sites _____

Videos _____

Books _____

Periodicals _____

Interviews _____

Comments _____

_____

Activities

GROUP MULTIMEDIA ACTIVITY

Pseudonyms and Famous Authors

Group _____

Name _____

Search the names of selected authors.

Name of author: _____

Pseudonym: _____

Search the dates of birth and death of famous author.

Birth: _____ Death: _____

Nationality: _____

Reason for pseudonyms or pen names: _____

_____

_____

_____

Each cooperative learning group will come up with a game like "Jeopardy" or "Author Bingo" and match the correct author's name with the correct pseudonym. Give each group five or more authors to search. Each group can play games that the other groups have created. Multimedia presentations, videos, or "Who Am I?" games are suggestions.

Suggested multimedia sources:

1. *Grolier Electronic Encyclopedia*
2. *Gale's Discovering Authors*
3. *Barron's Complete Book Notes*
4. *Compton's Interactive Encyclopedia*
5. *Monarch Notes*
6. *INFOTRAC*
7. *Humanities Index*

WORLD WIDE WEB SITES ON THE INTERNET

Academy One	http://nptn.org/cyber.serv/AOneP/
Children's Literature	http://www.ucalgary.ca/~dkbrown/index.html
Classroom Connect	http://www.wentworth.com/classroom/
EdWeb	http://K12.cnidr.org:90/
FIRN (Florida)	http://www.firn.edu/
Intercultural E-Mail	http://www.stolaf.edu/network/iecc/
K–12 Web Sites	http://www.sendit.nodak.edu/k12
KidPub	http://en-garde.com/kidpub/
Kids on the Web	http://www.zen.org/~brendan/kids.html
Kid's Web	http://www.npac.syr.edu/textbook/kidsweb/
Literature	http://portico.bl.UK/access/beowulf/ electronic-beowulf.html
Sites for Educators	http://www.mtjeff.com/~bodenst/page5.html
Thomas Web	http://thomas.loc.gov/
U.S. Dept. Education	http:/www.ed.gov/
U.S. Geological Survey	http://info.er.usgs.gov/
U.S. Presidents	http://www.fujisan.demon.co.uk/ uspresidents/preslist.htm
WebMuseum	http://www.oir.ucf.edu/louvre/
Yahoo	http://www.yahoo.com

Famous Pseudonyms

Writers can use pen names, or pseudonyms, for many reasons. Sometimes women use male names when their subject matter was not considered proper for women writers. Other authors have used fake names to avoid prosecution or anger about their work. And, of course, some authors just think it is fun. To help the teacher get started on the project, here is a list of authors who used pseudonyms.

Pseudonym	Author
Sholom Aleichem	Solom Rabinovitch
A.M. Barnard	Louisa May Alcott
Acton Bell	Anne Bronte
Currer Bell	Charlotte Bronte
Ellis Bell	Emily Bronte
Nicholas Blake	Cecil Day-Lewis
Nellie Bly	Elizabeth Cochraine Seaman
Boz	Charles Dickens
Max Brand	Frederick Faust
Ned Buntline	Edward Zane Carroll Judson
Lewis Carroll	Charles Lutwidge Dodgson
Manning Coles	Cyril Henry Coles
Susan Coolidge	Sarah Chauncey Woolsey
A.B. Cox; Francis Iles	Anthony Berkley
Edmund Crispin	Robert Bruce Montgomery
Amanda Cross	Carolyn Heilbrun
E.V. Cunningham	Howard Fast
Carter Dickson, Carr Dickson	John Dickson Carr
Isak Dinesen	Baroness Karen Blixen
Major Jack Downing	Seba Smith
Elia	Charles Lamb
George Eliot	Mary Ann (Marian) Evans
Paul Eluard	Eugene Grindel
A.A. Fair; Carleton Dendrake	Erle Stanley Gardner
Martha Farquharson	Martha Farquharson Finley
Fanny Fern	Sara Payson Willis
Maxim Gorky	Aleksey Maximovich Peshkov
Maxwell Gray	Mary Gleed Tuttiett
Knut Hamsun	Knut Pedersen

Pseudonym	Author
O. Henry	William Sidney Porter
Victoria Holt	Eleanor Burford Hibbert
Horace	Quintus Horatius Flaccus
Michael Innes	John Innes MacKintosh Stewart
Cyril Judd	Cyril M. Kornbluth
Kafiz	Shams-ud-din Muhammad
Carolyn Keene; Ralph Bonehill; Franklin W. Dixon; Arthur M. Winfield	Edward Stratemeyer
Diedrich Knickerbocker	Washington Irving
Emma Lathen	Mary J. Latis and Martha Hennissart
John Le Carre	David John Moore Cornwell
Richard Llewellyn	Richard Lloyd
Ed McBain	Evan Hunter
Hugh MacDiarmid	Christopher Murray Grieve
Ross MacDonald; John MacDonald	Kenneth Millar
Naquib Mahfouz	Abdel Aziz Al-Sabilgi
Katherine Mansfield	Kathleen Mansfield Beauchamp
J.J. Marric; Gordon Ashe; Robert Craine; Kyle Hunt; etc.	John Creasey
Andre Maurois	Emile Herzog
Judith Michael	Judith Barnard and Michael Fain
Yukio Mishima	Kimitake Hiraoka
Molière	Jean-Baptiste Poquelin
Pablo Neruda	Neftali Ricardo Reyes Basoalto
Frank O'Connor	Michael O'Donovan
George Orwell	Eric Arthur Blair
Lewis Padgett	Henry Kuttner
Pansy	Mrs. G.R. Alden
Peter Parley	Samuel Goodrich
Harry Patterson	Jack Higgins
Jean Paul	Johann Richter
Petrarch	Francesco Petrarca
Ellery Queen	Manford B. Lee—born Manford Lepofsky; and Frederick Dannay—born Daniel Nathan
Poor Richard	Benjamin Franklin

Pseudonym	Author
Sax Rohmer	Arthur Sarsfield Ward; also Arthur Sarsfield Wade
Jonathan Ryder	Robert Ludlum
Felix Summerly	Sir Henry Cole
Margaret Sydney	Harriet Mulford Lothrup
Mark Twain	Samuel Clemens
Elizabeth Wetherell	Susan Warner

Directions: The students can divide into groups of three or four per workstation and research specific authors and their pen names. They can search multimedia encyclopedias, *Wilson's Current Biography CD-ROM, Gale's Author Series on CD-ROM,* or the *World Wide Web*. They search for pseudonyms by typing in the author's name. They may want to research why the author chose that pen name. Could the students select a more appropriate pen name for the author?

Classic Authors

Real Name	Pen Name	Popular Works
Louisa May Alcott	A.M. Barnard	*Little Women*
Mrs. G.R. Alden	Pansy	*Aunt Hannah and Martha and John*
John Bunyan	none	*The Pilgrim's Progress*
Frances Hodgson Burnett	none	*Little Lord Fauntleroy; The Little Princess*
Samuel Clemens	Mark Twain	*Huckleberry Finn*
Sir Henry Cole	Felix Summerly	*Home Treasury Series*
Mary Elizabeth Dodge	none	*Hans Brinker*
Charles L. Dodgson	Lewis Carroll	*Alice in Wonderland*
Sarah Fielding	none	*The Governess, or Little Female Academy*
Martha Farquharson Finley	Martha Farquharson	*Elsie Dinsmore* series
Samuel Goodrich	Peter Parley	*Tale of Peter Parley About America*
Edward Lear	none	*Book of Nonsense*
Harriet Mulford Lothrup	Margaret Sydney	*The Five Little Peppers*
Susanna Rowson	none	*Charlotte Temple, A Tale of Truth*
Catherine Sedgwick	none	*A New England Tale*
Mrs. Sherwood	none	*The Fairchild Family*
Catherine Sinclair	none	*Holiday House*
Seba Smith	Major Jack Downing	*Way Down East, or Portraits of a Yankee Life*
Mary Gleed Tuttiett	Maxwell Gray	*The Silence of Dean Maitland*
Anna Warner	Amy Lothrup	*Dollars and Cents*
Susan Warner	Elizabeth Wetherell	*Wide, Wide World*
Sara Payson Willis	Fanny Fern	*Fern Leaves from Fanny's Portfolio*
Sara Chauncey Woolsey	Susan Coolidge	*What Katy Did* series
Charlotte Mary Yonge	none	*Heir of Redclyffe*

Directions: The teacher could give this list to students and leave out the "Pen Name," letting the students fill in the correct pen name.

Activity 2

STUDENT ACTIVITY: PSEUDONYMS

Authors have often chosen to write under assumed names or pseudonyms. You are given a list of famous authors who have used pseudonyms in the first column below. Your job is to match the pen names in the second column to the correct author.

Author	Pseudonym
1. William S. Porter	a. Mark Twain
2. Samuel L. Clemens	b. Poor Richard
3. Washington Irving	c. O. Henry
4. Benjamin Franklin	d. Jack Downing
5. Charles Lutwidge Dodgson	e. Boz
6. Louisa May Alcott	f. Diedrich Knickerbocker
7. Seba Smith	g. Currer Bell
8. C.D. Lewis	h. A.M. Barnard
9. Charles Dickens	i. Nicholas Blake
10. Charlotte Bronte	j. Lewis Carroll

Answers: 1-c, 2-a, 3-f, 4-b, 5-j, 6-h, 7-d, 8-i, 9-e, 10-g.

Activity 3

PRESIDENTIAL NICKNAMES

Nicknames of famous people are fun to study. Using multimedia resources investigate the background of United States presidents and match the president with the nickname. Choose a nickname from the list below and fill in the appropriate information about the president.

President's Name: _____

President's Nickname: _____

Reasons for Nickname: _____

_____

_____

List the resources used to complete the investigation: _____

_____

_____

Suggested Multimedia Resources:
   1995 Grolier Multimedia Encyclopedia CD-ROM
   It All Started with George CD-ROM
   U.S. Presidents CD-ROM
   The Software Toolworks Illustrated Encyclopedia CD-ROM

Presidential Nickname

 1. Honest Abe
 2. First Dark Horse
 3. The Rough Rider
 4. Ike
 5. Little Ben
 6. Father of the Constitution
 7. World Humanitarian
 8. Remember the Maine
 9. Old Rough and Ready
10. Napoleon of the Stump
11. Bleeding Kansas
12. Old Tippecanoe
13. Old Hickory
14. JFK
15. Old Buck
16. Atlas of Independence
17. Honest John
18. Big Bill
19. Old Veto
20. Accidental President
21. Jimmy
22. The Last Whig

Activity 4

FAMOUS AUTHORS' NICKNAMES

Nicknames of famous people are fun to study. Using multimedia resources investigate the background of famous authors and match the author with the nickname. Choose a nickname from the list given and fill in the appropriate information about the author.

Author's Name: _____

Author's Nickname: _____

Reasons for Nickname: _____

_____

_____

List the resources used to complete the investigation: _____

_____

_____

Could you create or think of a better nickname for the author. Explain why you chose this nickname: _____

_____

_____

Suggested multimedia:
    Gale's Discovering Authors
    Grolier Multimedia Encyclopedia
    Compton's Interactive Encyclopedia
    Monarch Notes
    INFOTRAC

    World Wide Web: Search Engines:
    Yahoo— http://www.yahoo.com/
    Lycos— http://www.lycos.com/
    AltaVista— http://www.altavista.digital.com:80/
    Literature— http://portico.bl.uk/access/beowulf/electronic-
      beowulf.html

Famous Nicknames

Authors

Aeschylus	Founder of Tragedies
Aristophanes	Father of Satire
Jane Austen	Masterful Miniaturist
Ambrose Bierce	Bitter Bierce
Anne Bradstreet	First Important Woman Writer in America
Max Brand	King of the Pulp Writers
Ned Buntline	Originator of Dime Novel
John Dickson Carr	Master of Locked Room Mysteries
Raymond Chandler	Master of Hard-Boiled Detective Stories
William Ellery Channing	Apostle of Unitarianism
G.K. Chesterton	Prince of Paradox
Gregory Corso	Renegade of American Poetry
Daniel Defoe	Father of Modern Journalism; Father of the English Novel (with Samuel Richardson)
Walter de la Mare	Poet of Childhood
Ralph Waldo Emerson	Sage of Concord
F. Scott Fitzgerald	Spokesman for the Lost Generation
Nathaniel Hawthorne	Gloomy Dean
O. Henry	Master of the Surprise Ending
Thomas Kyd	Father of English Tragedy (with Christopher Marlowe)
Joaquin Miller	Byron of Oregon
Edgar Allan Poe	Founder of Detective Stories and Thrillers
Joseph Pulitzer	Father of Modern American Journalism
James Whitcomb Riley	Poet of the Common People; Hoosier Poet
William Shakespeare	Best Writer of All Time; Bard of Albion
Tobias Smollett	Father of the Satirical Novel
Edmund Spenser	Poet's Poet
Jules Verne	The Man Who Invented the Future
Phillis Wheatley	First Important Black Poet in America
William Allen White	Sage of Emporia

The teacher may want to use this list to begin a research unit on famous people. Students could add to the list and have a contest to see who or which group could find the most famous nicknames. A database could be created and organized by the class.

Activity 5

Group name _____ Name _____

Famous places in literature have almost become as important to students as famous characters in literature. The "Mudville" setting for "Casey at the Bat" is perhaps as memorable as "Casey."

Many multimedia encyclopedias and multimedia literature CD-ROM resources will provide background information about literary places. Using the multimedia encyclopedia that is located in your classroom or library search the following places found in literature and write the name of the famous story that matches the setting.

Example:	**Famous Place**	**Famous Story**
	Mudville	Casey at the Bat
1.	Atlantis	_____
2.	Avalon	_____
3.	Blefuscu	_____
4.	Brobdingnag	_____
5.	Camelot	_____
6.	Forest of Arden	_____
7.	Gomorrah	_____
8.	Lilliput	_____
9.	Mount Olympus	_____
10.	Sleepy Hollow	_____
11.	Valhalla	_____
12.	Oz	_____
13.	Shangri-La	_____
14.	Parnassus	_____
15.	Never-Never Land	_____

Famous Places in Literature (Answers to Activity 5)

Atlantis   Legendary island located in the Atlantic Ocean.

Avalon   Island where King Arthur went at the end of his life.

Blefuscu (*Gulliver's Travels*)   Island north of Lilliput where the enemies of the Lilliputians lived.

Brobdingnag (*Gulliver's Travels*)   Where people are seventy feet tall.

Camelot   British site where King Arthur and the Knights of the Round Table met in legends.

Elysian Fields   Where the souls of good people went after death.

Forest of Arden   Setting of *As You Like It,* by Shakespeare.

Forest of Birnam   Where Macbeth's enemies disguise themselves using tree branches in Shakespeare's play.

Gomorrah   Biblical city that was destroyed because of its evil people.

Lilliput (*Gulliver's Travels*)   Where the people were only six inches tall.

Mount Olympus   Mythological home of the Greek gods.

Mudville   Setting for *Casey at the Bat.*

Never-Never Land (Neverland)   Where Peter Pan lives. No one ever grows up there.

Oz   The kingdom and home of Oz, a magician. Dorothy is carried there by a tornado.

Parnassus   Greek mountains where the Muses lived in mythology.

Shangri-La   A place of eternal youth and peace in *Lost Horizon.*

Sherwood Forest   The woods where Robin Hood and his Merry Men lived.

Sleepy Hollow   Village in *The Legend of Sleepy Hollow.*

Sodom   Biblical city destroyed because its people were evil.

Valhalla   Norse heaven for warriors who died in battle.

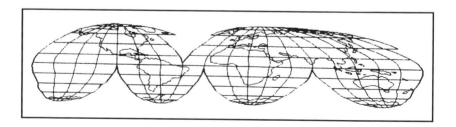

Activity 6

It is fun to search and find the author of famous quotations as well as the context of the quote. What did Benjamin Franklin mean when he said, "a penny saved is a penny earned"? Name the title of the book that Benjamin Franklin wrote which included this famous quote that future generations ponder and analyze. (*Poor Richard's Almanac* written by Benjamin Franklin has the famous quote "a penny saved is a penny earned.")

A teacher may use this famous quote before or after instruction to enhance the lesson objective. The student may use this quote for a creative writing assignment in a certain time period. Or the student could choose this quote to use in a history or economics class.

Sometimes, teachers or librarians can use quotes as trivia for a search activity. For example, the directions may read: Complete the following quote and write the name of the author: "Listen my children and you shall hear of the _____

_____

_____ "

Author: _____

Also, an "Across the Curriculum" assignment could be to ask the student to complete the quote, name the author, and link the quote to a time period and event.

Complete the following quotation and fill in the appropriate information.

Quotation: "Ask not what your country can do for you _____

_____

_____ "

Author: _____

Event: _____

Time period: _____

Students could work on projects similar to the one above in cooperative learning groups and see how many quotes (with background information) they could complete in a specific time limit. The students could also come up with their own quotes. Many creative thinking skills could be utilized in this quotation assignment using the CD-ROM quotation program to search for their famous quotation. Many multimedia programs and CD-ROM full text programs are on the market and the 1901 edition of *Bartlett's Familiar Quotations* is found on the superhighway at http://www.columbia.edu/acis/bartleby/bartlett/. Each group could create their own quote for specific time periods and produce a video portfolio. Use the following quotes and let the students use their creative thinking skills in their cooperative learning groups to produce a presentation using historical or creative quotations written by the students. Remember, multimedia technology has few limits.

"Ask not what your country can do for you..."

EXECUTIVE OFFICE OF THE PRESIDENT

World Wide Web
    http://www.whitehouse.gov/White_House/EOP/
html/couples.html
    http://www.whitehouse.gov/WH/welcome.html

Activity 7

FAMOUS QUOTATIONS

Quotation resources are usually arranged by subject and author. Choose selected quotations and find the name of the author.

1. Quotation:

_____

_____

_____

_____

2. Author of the Quote:

_____

_____

_____

3. Subject:

_____

_____

_____

_____

4. Multimedia Source:

_____

_____

_____

Famous Quotations

"A book of verses underneath the bough, a jug of wine, a loaf of bread — and thou beside me singing in the wilderness — oh, wilderness were paradise enow!"— Omar Khayyam, *Rubaiyat*

"A classic is a book that's stood the test of time, a book that men and women all over the world keep reaching for throughout the ages for its special enlightenment.... Classics open up your mind. Classics help you grow. Classics help you understand your life, your world, yourself."— Steve Allen

"A foolish consistency is the hobgoblin of little minds..."— Ralph Waldo Emerson, "Self Reliance"

"A little learning is a dangerous thing."— Alexander Pope, "An Essay on Criticism"

"A man's a man for a' that."— Robert Burns, "Is There for Honest Poverty"

"A man's reach should exceed his grasp."— Robert Browning, "Luria"

"A penny saved is a penny earned."— Ben Franklin, *Poor Richard's Almanac*

"'A picture is worth ten thousand words,' goes the time worn Chinese maxim. But one writer tartly said, 'It takes words to say that.'"— Leo Rosten

"A small leak will sink a great ship."— Ben Franklin, *Poor Richard's Almanac*

"A thing of beauty is a joy forever."— John Keats, "Endymion"

"A word is not a crystal, transparent and unchanged; it is the skin of all living thought and may vary greatly in color and content according to the circumstances and time in which it is used."— Oliver Wendell Holmes, Jr.

"All animals are equal, but some animals are more equal than others."— George Orwell, *Animal Farm*

"All for one and one for all."— Alexandre Dumas, *The Three Musketeers*

"All great speakers were bad speakers at first."— Ralph Waldo Emerson

"All is for the best in this best of all possible worlds."— Voltaire, *Candide*

"An iron curtain has descended across the continent."— Winston Churchill, speech on March 4, 1946

"And so, my fellow Americans, ask not what your country can do for you; ask what you can do for your country."— John F. Kennedy's inaugural address

"And therefore never send to know for whom the bell tolls; it tolls for thee."— John Donne, *Devotions Upon Emergent Occasions, Meditation XVII*

"Anyone can make history. Only a great man can write it."— Oscar Wilde

"Beauty is truth, truth is beauty — that is all ye know on earth, all ye need to know."— John Keats, "Ode on a Grecian Urn"

"Because I could not stop for death he kindly stopped for me..."— Emily Dickinson, "The Chariot"

"But I have promises to keep, and miles to go before I sleep..."— Robert Frost, "Stopping by Woods on a Snowy Evening"

"Call me Ishmael."— Herman Melville, *Moby Dick*

"Candy is dandy, but liquor is quicker."— Ogden Nash, "Reflections on Ice-Breaking"

"Cogito, ergo sum." ("I think; therefore I am.")— Rene Descartes, "Pensees," *Discours de la Methode (Part IV)*

"Come live with me and be my love."— Christopher Marlowe, "The Passionate Shepherd to His Love"

"Death, be not proud, though some have called thee mighty and dreadful for thou art not so..."— John Donne, "Death"

"Death always comes too early or too late."— *English Proverb*

"Do not go gentle into that good night. Rage, rage against the dying of the light."— Dylan Thomas, "Do Not Go Gentle Into That Good Night"

"Drink to me only with thine eyes."— Ben Jonson, "To Celia"

"East is east, and west is west, and never the twain shall meet."— Rudyard Kipling, "Ballad of East and West"

"Elementary."— Sir Arthur Conan Doyle, "The Crooked Man" and other Sherlock Holmes stories

"Far from the madding crowd's ignoble strife their sober wishes never learned to stray."— Thomas Gray, "Elegy Written in a Country Churchyard"

"Four score and seven years ago our fathers brought forth upon this continent a new nation..."— Abraham Lincoln, "Gettysburg Address"

"From the moment I picked your book up until I laid it down I was convulsed with laughter. Some day I intend reading it."— Groucho Marx

"Full many a flower is born to blush unseen and waste its sweetness on the desert air."— Thomas Gray, "Elegy Written in a Country Churchyard"

"Gather ye rosebuds while ye may."— Robert Herrick, "To the Virgins, to Make Much of Time"

"Give me your tired, your poor, your huddled masses yearning to breathe free, the wretched refuse of your teeming shore."— Emma Lazarus, "The New Colossus" (on the base of the Statue of Liberty)

"God bless us, every one!"— Charles Dickens, *A Christmas Carol*

"God's in his heaven—all's right with the world."—Robert Browning, "Pippa Passes"

"Good fences make good neighbors."—Robert Frost, "Mending Walls"

"Had we but world enough, and time, this coyness, lady, were no crime."—Andrew Marvell, "To His Coy Mistress"

"Happy families are all alike; every unhappy family is unhappy in its own way."—Leo Tolstoi, *Anna Karenina*

"He who, mixing grave and gay, can teach and yet give pleasure, gains a vote from each."—Horace, *De Arte Poetica*

"Home is the sailor, home from the sea, and the hunter home from the hill."—Robert Lewis Stevenson, "Requiem"

"How do I love thee? Let me count the ways."—Elizabeth Barrett Browning, "Sonnets from the Portuguese"

"I am the master of my fate; I am the captain of my soul."—William Ernest Henley, "Invictus"

"I celebrate myself, and sing myself."—Walt Whitman, *Leaves of Grass*

"I have a dream…"—Martin Luther King, Jr., "Lincoln Memorial Speech"

"I have nothing to offer, but blood, toil, tears, and sweat…"—Winston Churchill speech, May 13, 1940, House of Commons

"I never knew any man in my life who could not bear another's misfortunes perfectly like a Christian."—Alexander Pope, "Thoughts on Various Subjects"

"I think that I shall never see a poem lovely as a tree."—Joyce Kilmer, "Trees"

"I wandered lonely as a cloud."—William Wordsworth, "Daffodils"

"If you scoff at language study … how, save in terms of language, will you scoff?"—Mario Pei

"I'm nobody! Who are you? Are you nobody, too?"—Emily Dickinson untitled poem written in 1890

"In composing, as a general rule, run your pen through every other word you have written: you have no idea what vigor it will give your style."—Sydney Smith

"In doing what we ought we deserve no praise, because it is our duty."—St. Augustine

"In Flanders fields the poppies blow between the crosses row on row…"—John McCrae, "In Flanders Field"

"It is a far, far better thing I do, than I have ever done."—Charles Dickens, *A Tale of Two Cities*

"It is with narrow-souled people as with narrow-necked bottles; the less they have in them the more noise they make in pouring it out."—Alexander Pope, "Thoughts on Various Subjects"

"It was the best of times, it was the worst of times."— Charles Dickens, *A Tale of Two Cities*

"Jerusalem the golden, with milk and honey blest, Beneath thy contemplation sink heart and voice oppressed."— John Mason Neale

"Language develops by the felicitous misapplication of words."— J.B. Greenough

"Language is the dress of thought."— Samuel Johnson

"Learning language is not an abstract construction of the learned, or of dictionary makers, but is something arising out of the work, needs, ties, joys, affections, tastes, of long generations of humanity, and has its bases broad and low, close to the ground."— Walt Whitman

"Let him now speak, or else hereafter forever hold his peace."—*Book of Common Prayer of the Anglican Church*

"Listen my children, and you shall hear of the midnight ride of Paul Revere."— Henry Wadsworth Longfellow, "Paul Revere's Ride"

"Literature is man's written record of what it is like to be alive."—*unknown*

"Literature is news that stays news."— Ezra Pound

"No man is an island"— John Donne, *Devotions Upon Emergent Occasions, Meditation XVII*

"Nobody dast blame this man. A salesman is got to dream, boy. It comes with the territory."— Arthur Miller, *Death of a Salesman*

"Nobody is bound by any obligation unless it has first been freely accepted."— Ugo Betti

"Off with her head! Off with his head!"— Lewis Carroll, *Alice's Adventures in Wonderland*

"Oh, wad some pow'r the giftie gie us to see oursels as others see us!"— Robert Burns, "To a Louse"

"One cannot live with the dead; either we die with them or we make them live again. Or else we forget them."— Louis Martin-Chauffier

"One if by land, two if by sea"— Henry Wadsworth Longfellow, "Paul Revere's Ride"

"Open sesame!"— Anonymous, *Ali Baba and the Forty Thieves from Arabian Nights*

"People are complaining almost everywhere that the sense of duty is disappearing. How could it be otherwise since no one cares any more about his rights?"— Albert Camus

"Perhaps the best tribute you can pay someone who dies is to share his belief in life by putting your life ahead of his death."— Max Lerner

"Poems are made by fools like me, but only God can make a tree."— Joyce Kilmer, "Trees"

"Poetry is a kind of gasp, and there it is, a spark on the page. Fiction on the other hand, is like a swamp fire."— Joy Kogawa

"Rose is a rose is a rose is a rose."— Gertrude Stein, "Sacred Emily"

"Satire's my weapon, but I'm too discreet to run amuck, and tilt at all I meet."— Alexander Pope, "Imitations of Horace"

"Ships that pass in the night, and speak each other in passing..."— Henry Wadsworth Longfellow, "Elizabeth"

"Shoot, if you must, this old gray head, but spare your country's flag."— John Greenleaf Whittier, "Barbara Brietchie"

"Silence is golden."— *Swiss proverb*

"Slang is a language that rolls up its sleeves, spits on its hands and goes to work."— Carl Sandburg

"That government is best which governs least."— Henry David Thoreau, "Civil Disobedience"

"The appeal of writing is primarily the investigation of mystery."— Joyce Carol Oates

"The best laid schemes o' mice an' men gang aft a-ley..." (go oft awry)— Robert Burns, "To a Mouse"

"The classics are only primitive literature. They belong to the same class as primitive machinery and primitive music and primitive medicine."— Stephen Leacock

"The female of the species is more deadly than the male."— Rudyard Kipling, "The Female of the Species"

"The golden age, which a blind tradition has hitherto placed in the past, is before us."— C.H. Saint-Simon

"The land was ours before we were the land's"— Robert Frost, "The Gift Outright"

"The last pleasure in life is the sense of discharging our duty."— William Hazlitt

"The limits of my language stand for the limits of my world."— Ludwig Wittenstein

"The mass of men lead lives of quiet desperation."— Henry David Thoreau, *Walden*

"The most valuable of all talents is that of never using two words when one will do."— Thomas Jefferson

"The only thing we have to fear is fear itself."— Franklin Delano Roosevelt's inaugural address, March 3, 1933

"The paths of glory lead but to the grave."— Thomas Gray, "Elegy Written in a Country Churchyard"

"The reports of my death are greatly exaggerated."— Mark Twain (Samuel

Clemens) after U.S. newspapers published information about his death

"The world is too much with us."—William Wordsworth, "The World Is Too Much with Us"

"Theirs not to reason why, theirs but to do and die."—Alfred, Lord Tennyson, "The Brook"

"There is no frigate like a book to take us lands away..."—Emily Dickinson, "There Is No Frigate Like a Book"

"There is no joy in Mudville—mighty Casey has struck out."—Ernest Lawrence Thayer, "Casey at the Bat"

"They also serve who only stand and wait."—John Milton, "On His Blindness"

"Things fall apart; the center cannot hold..."—William Butler Yeats, "The Second Coming"

"Those who cannot remember the past are condemned to repeat it."—George Santayana, *The Life of Reason: Reason in Common Sense*

"'Tis better to have loved and lost than never to have loved at all."—Alfred, Lord Tennyson, "In Memoriam"

"To err is human, to forgive divine."—Alexander Pope, "An Essay on Criticism"

"True ease in writing comes from art, not chance, As those move easiest who have learned to dance."—Alexander Pope, "An Essay on Criticism"

"We should not argue when duty calls—we should act."—Sophocles

"What is the use of such terrible diligence as may tire themselves out with, if they always postpone their exchange of smiles with Beauty and Joy to cling to irksome duties and relations?"—Helen Keller

"Writing has power, but its power has no vector. Writers can stir the mind, but they can't direct it. Times change things, God changes things, the dictators change things, but writers can't change anything."—Isaac Bashevis Singer

"You never realize death until you realize love."—Katherine Butler Hathaway

Activity 8

___

Fictitious characters in literature are remembered more than the titles and authors of books where they were created. Students may sometimes connect characteristics of book characters to titles, authors, and time periods of literature. These characters are an excellent way to teach across the curriculum. Many multimedia programs (index) are available for preschool through adult literature. These program vary according to grade level and difficulty of subject matter.

There are many interactive CD-ROM books and web sites available for K–12. Below is a listing of famous characters from books and suggestions to utilize these fictitious characters to teach creative and cooperative learning across the curriculum.

LITERARY CHARACTERS
WHO AM I?

Several famous literary characters have written an introduction about themselves. Read each of the statements and try to decide the title and author of the book where they can be found.

1. I live right on the Mississippi River. Last night my friend Jim that I sort of like threw a brick through our window, but he really didn't mean it. Mark Twain was my creator. Who am I? _____

___

2. I'm about history's cruelest slave driver. I am very busy, and I haven't time for talk. I was put here to do a job for Mrs. Harriet Beecher Stowe. Who am I? _____

___

3. I created "An apple a day keeps the doctor away." Mr. Benjamin Franklin and I worked together, but he took all the credit for my work.

___

4. I have just had a very long nap. I am famous for my knowledge of elves and bowling. Mr. Washington Irving created me. _____

___

Famous Literary Characters

Ahab, Captain (*Moby Dick,* Melville)   Main character in Melville's *Moby Dick,* who is intent on capturing the whale.

Aladdin (*Arabian Nights*)   A genie appears every time Aladdin rubs his lamp and grants Aladdin's wishes.

Alice (*Alice in Wonderland* and *Through the Looking Glass,* Carroll)   Main character in Lewis Carroll's books.

Antonio (*The Merchant of Venice,* Shakespeare)   Character who is asked to give a pound of flesh to repay his debt to Shylock, the money lender.

Antony, Mark (*Antony and Cleopatra* and *Julius Caesar,* Shakespeare)   Mark Antony was a general and friend of Caesar who later became triumvir.

Baba, Ali (*Arabian Nights*)   Ali Baba opens the cave of gold by saying "Open sesame!"

Babar (*Babar,* de Brunhoff)   Elephant character in books by Jean and Laurent de Brunhoff.

Babbitt (*Babbitt,* Sinclair Lewis)   Real estate agent who puts money before all else.

Beast (*Beauty and the Beast*)   Ugly character who is loved by Beauty for his kind and loving behavior despite his appearance.

Beauty (*Beauty and the Beast*)   Beautiful female character who falls in love with the ugly Beast.

Beowulf (*Beowulf*)   Killed Grendel, the monster.

Black Beauty (*Black Beauty,* Sewell)   Horse in Anna Sewell's story.

Bones, Bram (*The Legend of Sleepy Hollow,* Irving)   Ichabod Crane's rival for the love of a young lady who tries to scare Crane.

Brer Fox (*Uncle Remus* stories)   Fox who usually loses to Brer Rabbit.

Brer Rabbit (Uncle Remus stories)   A rabbit who usually manages to outwit Brer Fox.

Brothers Karamazov (*Brothers Karamazov,* Dostoyevsky)   Ivan, Alyosha, Smerdyakov, and Dmitri. Dmitri is accused of murdering their father.

Brutus (*Julius Caesar,* Shakespeare)   Led the conspiracy against Caesar and murdered him.

Bumpo, Natty (*The Leatherstocking Tales,* Cooper)   Adopted the Indian way of living.

Butler, Rhett (*Gone with the Wind,* Mitchell)   Scarlett's third husband.

Casey ("Casey at the Bat," Thayer)   Bsaeball player who strikes out in the ninth inning.

Catherine (*Wuthering Heights*, Emily Bronte)   Character that Heathcliff loves obsessively.

Cheshire Cat (*Alice in Wonderland*, Carroll)   Cat that disappears with just his grin remaining visible.

Chicken Little (*Chicken Little*, fairy tale)   A chicken who tells everyone the sky is falling after being hit on the head by an acorn.

Christian (*The Pilgrim's Progress*, Bunyan)   Main male character in John Bunyan's allegory.

Cid, El (*Poem of Cid*)   Hero of the twelfth century Spanish epic.

Cinderella (*Cinderella*)   Fairy tale character who has two mean step-sisters and a step-mother.

Cleopatra (*Antony and Cleopatra*, Shakespeare)   Queen of Egypt.

Copperfield, David (*David Copperfield*, Dickens)   Main character in Dickens' story about cruel treatment to British children.

Cordelia (*King Lear*, Shakespeare)   Only daughter of King Lear who truly loves him.

Cowardly Lion (*The Wonderful Wizard of Oz*, Baum)   A lion who seeks courage from the wizard.

Crane, Ichabod (*The Legend of Sleepy Hollow*, Irving)   Schoolteacher who is frightened by the Headless Horseman.

Cratchit, Bob (*Christmas Carol*, Dickens)   Worked for Scrooge and was Tiny Tim's father.

Crusoe, Robinson (*Robinson Crusoe*, Defoe)   Character shipwrecked on an island for years.

d'Artagnan (*The Three Musketeers*, Dumas)   A friend of the musketeers Porthos, Athos, and Aramis.

Desdemona (*Othello*, Shakespeare)   Wife that Othello kills in a jealous rage.

Dorothy (Gale) (*The Wonderful Wizard of Oz*, Baum)   A girl who finds herself in an enchanted kingdom looking for a way home to Kansas.

Dracula, Count (*Count Dracula*, Stoker)   A vampire.

Emile (*Emile*, Rousseau)   Character in a book that was intended to illustrate how a boy should be educated.

Fagin (*Oliver Twist*, Dickens)   Teaches Oliver and other boys how to be pickpockets.

Falstaff (*King Henry the Fourth*, Shakespeare)   A lovable rogue.

Faust   Magician and alchemist in plays by Christopher Marlowe and Goethe.

Figaro (*The Marriage of Figaro*, Mozart and *The Barber of Seville*, Rossini) Spanish barber created by Beaumarchais.

Finn, Huckleberry (*The Adventures of Huckleberry Finn*, Twain) An orphan who has adventures with a runaway slave.

Fogg, Phineas (*Around the World in Eighty Days*, Verne) Character in Jules Verne's novel.

Frankenstein, Dr. Victor (*Frankenstein*, Shelley) Scientist who creates a monster.

Friar Tuck (*Robin Hood*) One of Robin's faithful men.

Friday (*Robinson Crusoe*, Defoe) Robinson Crusoe's companion.

Gatsby, Jay (*The Great Gatsby*, Fitzgerald) Man who tries to win back the heart of his sweetheart after becoming rich.

Goldilocks (*The Three Bears*) Girl who goes into a bear family's house and uses their things.

Goody Two-Shoes (*Goody Two-Shoes*, Goldsmith) A poor girl who is given shoes to make her happy.

Gradgrind (*Hard Times*, Dickens) Utilitarian who comes to see the error in his ways.

Gretel (*Hansel and Gretel*) Gretel and her brother Hansel come upon a witch in a gingerbread house while wondering through the woods.

The Grinch (*How the Grinch Stole Christmas*, Dr. Seuss) Misery character who tries to ruin everyone's Christmas.

Gulliver (*Gulliver's Travels*, Swift) Character who travels to four different places as Swift mocks human frailties.

Hamlet (*Hamlet*, Shakespeare) Avenges the murder of his father by killing the murderer, his Uncle Claudius.

Hansel (*Hansel and Gretel*) He and his sister Gretel come upon a witch in a gingerbread house while wondering through the woods.

Hawkins, Jim (*Treasure Island*, Stevenson) Boy who causes troubles for a group of pirates.

Heathcliff (*Wuthering Heights*, Emily Bronte) Male character who is obsessed with Catherine.

Heep, Uriah (*David Copperfield*, Dickens) A blackmailer.

Holmes, Sherlock (stories by Doyle) Famous cunning detective who solves the most difficult of mysteries.

Hook, Captain (*Peter Pan*) Evil pirate who had a hook for a hand after it was eaten by a crocodile.

Humpty Dumpty (Nursery rhyme and *Through the Looking Glass*) Egg who falls off a wall.

Hyde, Mr. (*The Strange Case of Dr. Jekyll and Mr. Hyde*, Stevenson)   Dr. Jekyll's evil side who comes out after drinking a potion.

Iago (*Othello*, Shakespeare)   Soldier who tricks Othello.

Jeeves   Butler, in P.G. Wodehouse's writings.

Jekyll, Dr. (*The Strange Case of Dr. Jekyll and Mr. Hyde*, Stevenson) Character who experiments on himself.

Jim (*The Adventures of Huckleberry Finn*, Twain)   The escaped slave who travels down river with Huckleberry Finn.

Juan, Don (Lord Byron poem and *Man and Superman*, Shaw)   A notorious woman chaser also known as Don Giovanni.

Juliet (*Romeo and Juliet*, Shakespeare)   A young female who loves Romeo, but their families are feuding.

Legree, Simon (*Uncle Tom's Cabin*, Stowe)   Cruel slave driver.

Lennox, Mary (*The Secret Garden*, Burnett)   A girl who finds happiness tending an overgrown garden.

Little John (*Robin Hood*)   One of Robin's Merry Men.

Loman, Willie (*Death of a Salesman*, Miller)   An unhappy character who eventually commits suicide.

Macawber (*David Copperfield*, Dickens)   A secondary character in the novel.

Macbeth (*Macbeth*, Shakespeare)   Character who murdered the king to gain the throne of Scotland for himself.

Malaprop, Mrs. (*The Rivals*, Sheridan)   Character who continuously mixes up similar words.

March Hare (*Alice's Adventures in Wonderland*, Carroll)   Character in Lewis Carroll's story.

March Sisters (Meg, Jo, Beth, Amy) (*Little Women*, Alcott)   The four sisters who are the main characters in the book.

Mitty, Walter (*The Secret Life of Walter Mitty*, Thurber)   Character who lives in a fantasy world.

Mother Goose   Nursery rhymes are attributed to her.

Mowgli (*Jungle Book*, Kipling)   Indian boy who is raised by a pack of wolves.

O'Hara, Scarlett (*Gone with the Wind*, Mitchell)   Southern belle who lives through the Civil War.

Othello (*Othello*, Shakespeare)   Believed that his wife was unfaithful and killed her only to find that he was tricked.

Pan, Peter (*Peter Pan*, Barrie)   A boy who never grows up.

Panza, Sancho (*Don Quixote*, Cervantes)   Don Quixote's sidekick.

Pickwick, Samuel (*The Pickwick Papers*, Dickens)   Character who uses words in strange ways.

Pied Piper of Hamlin ("Pied Piper of Hamlin," Browning)   Plays his flute to lure rats from town and enchants children when the people fail to pay him his due.

Pinocchio (*Pinocchio*, Collodi)   A wooden puppet who wants to be a real boy. His nose grows larger each time he tells a lie.

Pip (*Great Expectations*, Dickens)   A boy who leaves his real friends because he is consumed with ambition.

Pollyanna (*Pollyanna*, Porter)   Girl who remains happy and cheerful through many rough times.

Portia (*The Merchant of Venice*, Shakespeare)   Female character who saves Shylock from paying the utmost price for his debt.

Prospero (*The Tempest*, Shakespeare)   Banished to an island and rules with magic.

Prynne, Hester (*Scarlet Letter*, Hawthorne)   Woman forced to wear a scarlet A on her dress to signify adultery.

Puck (*A Midsummer Night's Dream*, Shakespeare)   A mischievous fairy.

Puss in Boots (*Puss in Boots*, fairy tale)   A cat who wore red boots and tried to win the princess' hand for his master through clever tricks.

Quasimodo (*The Hunchback of Notre Dame*, Hugo)   A hunchbacked bell-ringer.

Quixote, Don (*Don Quixote*, de Cervantes)   Adventurer who makes a fool of himself during his escapades.

Rapunzel (*Rapunzel*, fairy tale)   Female character who was given to a witch and had long, beautiful hair that a prince used to climb the tower the witch kept her in.

Red Riding Hood   Fairy tale heroine who is tricked by a wolf pretending to be her grandmother.

Rip Van Winkle (*Rip Van Winkle*, Irving)   A character who goes hunting, falls asleep for 20 years, and returns home.

Robin, Christopher (Milne's series of books)   The boy who owns Winnie-the-Pooh.

Romeo (*Romeo and Juliet*, Shakespeare)   He was in love with Juliet but their families were feuding.

Rowland, Childe   King Arthur's youngest son who searches for his sister, Burd Ellen, with the help of Merlin.

Rumpelstiltskin (*Rumpelstiltskin*, fairy tale)   Dwarf who helps a princess spin straw into gold.

Samsa, Gregor ("The Metamorphosis," Kafka)   Character who is changed into a giant insect.

Sawyer, Tom (*Tom Sawyer*, Twain)   A boy who continuously gets into trouble.

Scarecrow (*The Wonderful Wizard of Oz*, Baum)   Character who asks the wizard to give him a brain.

Scheherazade (*Arabian Nights*)   Queen who told 1001 stories to her husband.

Scrooge, Ebenezer (*A Christmas Carol*, Dickens)   Miser who is famous for "Bah, humbug." He is visited by three ghosts who try to change his heart at Christmas.

Seven Dwarfs (*The Seven Dwarfs*, Disney film)   Happy, Bashful, Dopey, Sneezy, Grumpy, Doc, and Sleepy.

Sharp, Becky (*Vanity Fair*, Thackeray)   Female character who obtains wealth and power by any means.

Shylock (*The Merchant of Venice*, Shakespeare)   A money-lender who demands impossible paybacks.

Silver, Long John (*Treasure Island*, Stevenson)   Pirate who searches for treasures.

Sinbad the Sailor (*Arabian Nights*)   Main character in "The History of Sinbad the Sailor."

Sleeping Beauty (*Sleeping Beauty*)   Princess who is put under a spell to sleep for 100 years unless a handsome prince kisses her.

Snow White (*Snow White and the Seven Dwarfs*, fairy tale)   A beautiful young girl who is poisoned by her wicked stepmother.

Superman (*Superman*, comic)   A super hero who fights crime and injustice with his super human powers. He can fly, "run faster than a speeding bullet," and "leap tall buildings in a single bound."

Tarzan (*Tarzan*, comic book)   A hero who was raised by apes in an African jungle.

Thatcher, Becky (*Tom Sawyer*, Twain)   Tom Sawyer's girlfriend.

Tin Woodman (*The Wonderful Wizard of Oz*, Baum)   Character who seeks a heart from the Wizard.

Tinker Bell (*Peter Pan*)   Fairy who teaches Peter Pan how to fly.

Tiny Tim (*A Christmas Carol*, Dickens)   A young, crippled boy who is helped in the end by Scrooge.

Toad (*Wind in the Willows*, Grahame)   A playboy who is helped by friends, Mole, Rat and Badger. They find peace to the wind's song in the trees.

Tom Thumb (*Tom Thumb*, fairy tale)   A tiny boy no bigger than a thumb.

Tweedledum and Tweedledee (*Through the Looking Glass*, Carroll) Overweight twins who meet Alice.

Twist, Oliver (*Oliver Twist*, Dickens) Orphaned character who finds himself in a workhouse, abused, and in a gang before coming out all right.

Uncle Remus (Uncle Remus stories) African-American storyteller who tells stories using animals for characters.

Uncle Tom (*Uncle Tom's Cabin*, Stowe) A mistreated slave.

Watson (Sherlock Holmes' series, Conan Doyle) Sherlock Holmes' sidekick.

White Knight (*Through the Looking Glass*, Carroll) The White Knight was supposed to help Alice cross the next brook but she kept him from falling off his horse.

White Rabbit (*Alice's Adventures in Wonderland*, Carroll) The rabbit Alice chases into Wonderland.

Winnie-the-Pooh (Milne series) A toy bear.

Wizard of Oz (*The Wonderful Wizard of Oz*, Baum) A character who pretends to be brave and powerful and to give Dorothy and her friends what they are seeking.

Suggested Activities: Students can create their own "Who Am I?" literary characters. They can research a character from the list and write their own description or they can choose a favorite character from a book they have read. Students could also make a video and dress up like the character. Art work and animation could be used on a "Who Am I?" slide presentation (PowerPoint) to the class.

Sharing Books with Multimedia

Young and old alike enjoy sharing favorite books. In the 21st century classrooms educators can still use traditional methods of motivating students to read utilizing multimedia technology. There will always be those students who will have tattered paperbacks in their pockets and will be reading in a corner of a classroom or library as others are searching the Web or CD-ROM databases for their favorite author. Below is a list of ways to share a book. Educators can use these suggestions with the Multimedia Book List and Web sites which follows. Remember to always check the Web sites weekly to see if the addresses have changed. An excellent technical book entitled *Absolute Beginner's Guide to Multimedia* by Ron Wodaski (Sams Publishing) presents a step-by-step approach to manipulating video and audio for presentations. These activities can be utilized with cooperative learning groups or individual students.

Share a Book

Dramatize a mystery from a favorite book, video the dramatization, and produce a multimedia presentation using selected parts of the video to interact with the audience letting the audience decide what happened or who did it. If time doesn't permit the dramatization of the story, dramatize what happened and interact with the audience with discussion of what circumstances could have made it happen.

Make a list of facts from a favorite book. Analyze the information and decide if it is actually fact or fiction. A discussion of "How to be able to distinguish between fact and fiction" is pertinent when utilizing multimedia in the classroom or library.

Using a courtroom approach students will take opposing viewpoints and persuade an audience to read or not read a book by a creative book review. Using the *INFOTRAC* or *Wilson's Readers' Guide to Periodical Literature* on CD-ROM or other electronic resources find the following information for your review: name of author, title of the book, publication date, publisher, setting, genre and any other information which helps simplify the review. Utilize video clips, audio, or multimedia clips to reinforce your review. Closing arguments must be creative and inventive to convince the audience to read or not read the book!

Write a poem about a character and use PowerPoint (or another program) to present it to an audience. Students could be divided into groups and be given specific assignments such as editor, producer, director, writer, illustrator, reader, and any other job description needed. Students could add music, sound effects, and their own special creative effects to the production. This could be a year-long activity and poetry could be added continuously throughout the year. At the end of the year the class would have their own Poetry Database which they produced.

Create games such as Bingo, Jeopardy, crossword puzzles, and projects such as timelines, models, songwriting, mural, puppets, or video interviews about a favorite book using a combination of media. Have a book festival to enjoy the inventions.

Projects on the Internet

Newsgroups are a collection of messages which are organized into subjects and posted on the Internet. To read or post a message the provider must have a news reader. Most state departments of education or education providers have a news reader. Below are several newsgroups which may offer students the opportunity to share information on a school project.

Group	Subject
k12.chat.elementary	conversations for elementary students
k12.chat.junior	conversations for grades 6–8
k12.chat.senior	conversations for high school students

World Wide Web Search Tools
Kids on the Web
http://www.zen.org/brendan/kids.html
Kids Web
http://www.npac.syr.edu/textbook/kidsweb

The following "Favorite Book Poll" can be presented via the Internet. Telecommunication skills are practiced and reinforced. Comparisons can be made between ages, geographical areas, cultures, and others.

Favorite Book Poll

Name _____

Grade _____

State/Country _____

Please list your three favorite books you have recently read. List them in order of most favorite first, then second favorite, and third.

1. _____

2. _____

3. _____

Comments: _____

_____

Multimedia Book List

(see resources on pages 101–143)

Aesop's Fables
Annabel's Dream of Ancient Egypt
Beauty and the Beast
Beauty and the Beast: A Multimedia Storybook
The Bible Library
Children's Favorite Stories, Poems, and Fairy Tales
Children's Treasury of Stories, Nursery Rhymes, and Songs
Cinderella
Classic Library
Discis
Don Quixote
Favorite Folk Tales
Heather Hits Her First Home Run
Interactive Storytime, Volumes 1 and 3
Just Grandma and Me
Library of the Future Series
A Long Hard Day on the Ranch
Mixed-Up Mother Goose
Moving Gives Me a Stomach Ache
Mud Puddle
The Myths and Legends of Ancient Greece
The Night Before Christmas
Oxford Shakespeare
Peter and the Wolf
Project Gutenberg
The Reading Carnival
Reading Short Stories
Scary Poems for Rotten Kids
Shakespeare
Sherlock Holmes: Consulting Detective Vol. 3
Sherlock Holmes on Disc
A Silly Noisy House
The Sleeping Beauty
Story Time
The Tale of Benjamin Bunny
The Tale of Peter Rabbit
Talking Classic Tales
Thomas' Snowsuit
Twain's World
The Whale of a Tale
World Library Great Mystery Classics
World Library Great Poetry Classics
World Library Greatest Books Collection
World Literary Heritage

World Wide Web Resources for Books

The Project Gutenberg (All ages)
http://jg.cso.uiuc.edu/PG/welcome.html

Children's Literature Web Guide (All ages — Children, Parents, Educators)
http://www.ucalgary.ca/~dkbrown/index.html

Postcard Store (All ages)
http://postcards.www.media.mit.edu/Postcards/

Kids' Space (Ages 5–10)
http://plaza/interport.net/kids_space

I-Site.On.Canada (All ages)
http://i-site.on.ca/default.html#Fables

The Reading Room (All ages)
http://www.inform.umd.edu:8080/EdRes/ReadingRoom

KidPub (All ages)
http://en-garde.com/kidpub
(Students may write to authors)

Activity 10

MULTIMEDIA RESEARCH TIME

Group_____

Name_____

Choose one of the following topics, research it, and create a video or interactive, multimedia presentation of the collectibles.

Choose one of the following kinds of collectibles and prove that the collectibles are either a good or a bad investment. Narrow the topic into specific namebrands if possible.

Postmarks	Stamps	Campaign Buttons
Olympic Pins	Hub Caps	Matchbook Covers
Comic Books	Dolls	Sugar Wrappers
Baseball Cards	Teacups	Model Trains
Toy Soldiers	Faberge Eggs	Matchbox Cars
Spoons	Books	Golden Books
Thimbles	Lunch Boxes	Star Trek "Stuff"
Jukeboxes	Jewelry	Glass

Research fads and add to the following list.

Troll Dolls	Haircuts (Mohawks)	Bumper Stickers
"Smile Buttons"	Hoola Hoops	Skateboards

Research the history of a familiar product or object. Add to the following list.

Swatch Watch	Crayola Crayons	Slinky
Lego Blocks	McDonald's	Coke
Crossword Puzzles	Lincoln Logs	Etch a Sketch

Multimedia resources:

1. *INFOTRAC*
2. *Readers' Guide to Periodical Literature Abstracts*
3. *Compton's Interactive Encyclopedia*
4. *Wilsondisc/Business Periodical Index with Text*

Activity 11

BASIC GUIDE FOR USING WILSONDISC

Business Periodicals Index
Humanities Index
Applied Science & Technology Index

1. If the display is a
   - blank red screen, press *enter* (display)
   - blue screen with a subject box at the bottom, type in the subject and *enter* (display)
   - list of data left by previous user, follow directions at bottom of screen

2. If there are no citations for your subject, press *see also* (F8), then type in the suggested term and press *enter* (display)

Remember:
Check to see if the periodical is available:
BOUND   go to the stacks — Bound Journal Section
UNBOUND   go the Circulation Desk
MICROFICHE   go to the Microfiche Readers and Cabinet

If the library/media center doesn't have the periodical ask the librarian or media specialist if it can be retrieved through the World Wide Web.

Ask a librarian for help at any point in your search.

Activity 12

NEWBERY MEDAL BOOKS/ROUND TABLE

Group_____

Name_____

    Each group will select an author who has received a Newbery Award from the list. The students will read separate books written by the same author. The team will have time to read, discuss, and complete the questionnaire about the book. Then, the groups will meet together and share highlights of their discussions with the class or participants. The group may want to make a multimedia presentation, drama, video, or other media to share their common highlight about their author. Hopefully, these activities will encourage all participants to read.

    Students can access information about Newbery Medal Books and Caldecott Medal Books through the Internet. The following search engines will let the student type in a main subject such as NEWBERY or CALDECOTT and retrieve book reviews, Newbery medal book listings, honor books, and background information on both awards.

SEARCH ENGINES

Alta Vista http://altavista.digital.com
Excite http://www.excite.com
Lycos http://www.lycos.com
InfoSeek http://guide.infoseek.com
Opentext http://www.opentext.com.8080
Inktomi http://inktomi.berkeley.edu/query.html
WWW Worm http://www.cs.colorado.edu/wwww/
Webcrawler http://www.webcrawler.com

Newbery Round Table Discussion

A Newbery round table discussion can be a social and educational experience. The purpose in promoting a Newbery round table discussion is to encourage the enjoyment of reading and to solicit different view points concerning the interpretation of literature.

Different approaches can be used in a Newbery round table discussion. Participants can all read one book, then meet together to discuss certain aspects of that book. Or participants can all read books written by the same author. The latter approach helps the readers see a wider range of the writer's style and enables the reader to develop an appreciation and understanding of that writer's works. To stay active and alert, a person needs to keep interpreting information for himself. A person must think critically when he reads. Reading keeps the mind active and helps a person stay focused. Doing things like participating in a Newbery round table discussion helps you reflect, stimulates your ability to analyze people, and shows you how to cross over to other areas of interest.

This Newbery round table discussion is a non-threatening, motivational tool that will encourage reading, enhance social awareness, and develop an appreciation of literature.

Guidelines

Participants should first meet and make a decision about a writer to explore.

1. A large group might be given an opportunity to mingle, so that individuals can find other people who are interested in the same type of literature.
2. Participants might make a trip together to a local library in order to find the books that they have decided to read.
3. Each group of three to five people will read books by the same author; each person within each group will read a different book by that writer. For instance one group might chose the writer Louis L'Amour; one person might read *The Sacketts*; and another person might read *Jubal Sackett*; and another might read *The Californios*.
4. Participants should be given a certain amount of time to read their book.
5. It might be helpful for each participant to complete the questionnaire about his book found in Activity 13.

6. Each group should meet and discuss how all of the books are similar and different.
7. Each group will share the highlights of their discussion with all participants.

Activity 13

QUESTIONNAIRE

Where and when did your novel take place? _____

_____

What were the most important events (plot)? _____

_____

Describe a major or minor character (characterization). Think about his: personality, physical characteristics, interests, interaction with others, problems, etc. _____

_____

Is the major problem (conflict) in the story Man vs. Man, Man vs. Himself, Man vs. Society, Man vs. Nature, or Man vs. Fate? Explain. _____

_____

What do you think is the universal meaning (theme) of the book (example: friendship, love, survival, greed, etc.)? _____

_____

Would this writer's style fit into a certain genre (category of writing like mystery, romance, western, etc.)? Why? _____

_____

What did you learn from this Round Table Discussion that you didn't know before? _____

_____

Discuss positive and negative reactions to the books.

Positive: _____

_____

Negative: _____

_____

Activity 14

ROUND TABLE CRITIQUE FORM

This form could be completed by members of the audience.

Name of Participants	Title of Books	Theme	Comments
1.			
2.			
3.			
4.			
5.			
1.			
2.			
3.			
4.			
5.			
1.			
2.			
3.			
4.			
5.			

Newbery Medal Books

1922 Hendrik Wiliem van Loon, *The Story of Mankind*
1923 Hugh Lofting, *The Voyages of Dr. Dolittle*
1924 Charles Hawes, *The Dark Frigate*
1925 Charles Finger, *Tales from Silver Lands*
1926 Arthur Bowie Chrisman, *Shen of the Sea*
1927 Will James, *Smoky, the Cowhorse*
1928 Dhan Gopal Mukerji, *Gay-Neck, the Story of a Pigeon*
1929 Eric P. Kelly, *The Trumpeter of Krakow*
1930 Rachel Field, *Hitty, Her First Hundred Years*
1931 Elizabeth Coatsworth, *The Cat Who Went to Heaven*
1932 Laura Adams Armer, *Waterless Mountain*
1933 Elizabeth Lewis, *Young Fu of the Upper Yangtze*
1934 Cornelia Meigs, *Invincible Louisa*
1935 Monica Shannon, *Dobry*
1936 Carol Ryrie Brink, *Caddie Woodlawn*
1937 Ruth Sawyer, *Roller Skates*
1938 Kate Seredy, *The White Stag*
1939 Elizabeth Enright, *Thimble Summer*
1940 James Daugherty, *Daniel Boone*
1941 Armstrong Sperry, *Call It Courage*
1942 Walter D. Edmonds, *The Matchlock Gun*
1943 Elizabeth Janet Gray, *Adam of the Road*
1944 Esther Forbes, *Johnny Tremain*
1945 Robert Lawson, *Rabbit Hill*
1946 Lois Lenski, *Strawberry Girl*
1947 Carolyn Sherwin Bailey, *Miss Hickory*
1948 William Pène Du Bois, *The Twenty-One Balloons*
1949 Marguerite Henry, *King of the Wind*
1950 Marguerite de Angeli, *The Door in the Wall*
1951 Elizabeth Yates, *Amos Fortune, Free Man*
1952 Eleanor Estes, *Ginger Pye*
1953 Ann Nolan Clark, *Secret of the Andes*
1954 Joseph Krumgold, *…And Now Miguel*
1955 Meindert DeJong, *The Wheel on the School*
1956 Jean Lee Latham, *Carry On, Mr. Bowditch*
1957 Virginia Sorensen, *Miracles on Maple Hill*
1958 Harold Keith, *Rifles for Watie*
1959 Elizabeth George Speare, *The Witch of Blackbird Pond*

1960 Joseph Krumgold, *Onion John*
1961 Scott O'Dell, *Island of the Blue Dolphins*
1962 Elizabeth George Speare, *The Bronze Bow*
1963 Madeleine L'Engle, *A Wrinkle in Time*
1964 Emily Cheney Neville, *It's Like This, Cat*
1965 Maia Wojciechowska, *Shadow of a Bull*
1966 Elizabeth Borton de Trevino, *I, Juan de Pareja*
1967 Irene Hunt, *Up a Road Slowly*
1968 E.L. Konigsburg, *From the Mixed-Up Files of Mrs. Basil E. Frankweiler*
1969 Lloyd Alexander, *The High King*
1970 William H. Armstrong, *Sounder*
1971 Betsy Byars, *Summer of the Swans*
1972 Robert C. O'Brien, *Mrs. Frisby and the Rats of NIMH*
1973 Jean Craighead George, *Julie of the Wolves*
1974 Paula Fox, *The Slave Dancer*
1975 Virginia Hamilton, *M.C. Higgins, the Great*
1976 Susan Cooper, *The Grey King*
1977 Mildred D. Taylor, *Roll of Thunder, Hear My Cry*
1978 Katherine Paterson, *Bridge to Terabithia*
1979 Ellen Raskin, *The Westing Game*
1980 Joan W. Blos, *A Gathering of Days*
1981 Katherine Paterson, *Jacob Have I Loved*
1982 Nancy Williard, *A Visit to William Blake's Inn: Poems for Innocent and Experienced Travelers*
1983 Cynthia Voigt, *Dicey's Song*
1984 Beverly Cleary, *Dear Mr. Henshaw*
1985 Robin McKinley, *The Hero and the Crown*
1986 Patricia MacLachlan, *Sarah, Plain and Tall*
1987 Sid Fleischman, *The Whipping Boy*
1988 Russell Freedman, *Lincoln: A Photobiography*
1989 Paul Fleischman, *Joyful Noise: Poems for Two Voices*
1990 Lois Lowry, *Number the Stars*
1991 Jerry Spinelli, *Maniac Magee*
1992 Phyllis Reynolds Naylor, *Shiloh*
1993 Cynthia Rylant, *Missing May*
1994 Lois Lowry, *The Giver*
1995 Sharon Creech, *Walk Two Moons*
1996 Karen Cushman, *The Midwife's Apprentice*

Caldecott Medal Books (Illustrator is given for each work)

1938 Dorothy P. Lathrop, *Animals of the Bible* (text selected by Helen Dean Fish)

1939 Thomas Handforth, *Mei Li*

1940 Ingri and Edgar Parin d'Aulaire, *Abraham Lincoln*

1941 Robert Lawson, *They Were Strong and Good*

1942 Robert McCloskey, *Make Way for Ducklings*

1943 Virginia Lee Burton, *The Little House*

1944 Louis Slobodkin, *Many Moons* (text by James Thurber)

1945 Elizabeth Orton Jones, *Prayer for a Child* (text by Rachel Field)

1946 Maud and Miska Petersham, *The Rooster Crows*

1947 Leonard Weisgard, *The Little Island* (text by Golden MacDonald)

1948 Roger Duvoisin, *White Snow, Bright Snow* (text by Alvin Tresselt)

1949 Berta and Elmer Hader, *The Big Snow*

1950 Leo Politi, *Song of the Swallows*

1951 Katherine Milhous, *The Egg Tree*

1952 Nicolas Mordvinoff, *Finders Keepers* (text by William Lipkind)

1953 Lynd Ward, *The Biggest Bear*

1954 Ludwig Bemelmans, *Madeline's Rescue*

1955 Marcia Brown, *Cinderella, or the Little Glass Slipper*

1956 Feodor Rojankovsky, *Frog Went a-Courtin'* (retold by John Langstaff)

1957 Marc Simont, *A Tree Is Nice* (text by Janice Udry)

1958 Robert McCloskey, *Time of Wonder*

1959 Barbara Cooney, *Chanticleer and the Fox*

1960 Marie Hall Ets, *Nine Days to Christmas* (text by Marie Hall Ets and Aurora Labastida)

1961 Nicolas Sidjakov, *Baboushka and the Three Kings* (text by Ruth Robbins)

1962 Marcia Brown, *Once a Mouse*

1963 Ezra Jack Keats, *The Snowy Day*

1964 Maurice Sendak, *Where the Wild Things Are*

1965 Beni Montresor, *May I Bring a Friend?* (text by Beatrice Schenk de Regniers)

1966 Nonny Hogrogian, *Always Room for One More* (text by Sorche Nic Leodhas)

1967 Evaline Ness, *Sam, Bangs and Moonshine*

1968 Ed Emberley, *Drummer Hoff* (text by Barbara Emberley)

1969 Uri Shulevitz, *The Fool of the World and the Flying Ship* (retold by Arthur Ransome)

1970　William Steig, *Sylvester and the Magic Pebble*
1971　Gail E. Haley, *A Story, A Story: An African Tale*
1972　Nonny Hogrogian, *One Fine Day*
1973　Blair Lent, *The Funny Little Woman* (retold by Arlene Mosel)
1974　Margot Zemach, *Duffy and the Devil* (retold by Harve Zemach)
1975　Gerald McDermott, *Arrow to the Sun*
1976　Leo and Diane Dillon, *Why Mosquitoes Buzz in People's Ears* (retold by Verna Aardema)
1977　Leo and Diane Dillon, *Ashanti to Zulu: African Traditions* (text by Margaret Musgrove)
1978　Peter Spier, *Noah's Ark*
1979　Paul Goble, *The Girl Who Loved Wild Horses*
1980　Barbara Cooney, *Ox-Cart Man*
1981　Arnold Lobel, *Fables*
1982　Chris Van Allsburg, *Jumanji*
1983　Marcia Brown, *Shadow* (text by Blaise Cendrars)
1984　Alice and Martin Provensen, *The Glorious Flight: Across the Channel with Louis Blériot*
1985　Trina Schart Hyman, *Saint George and the Dragon* (retold by Margaret Hodges)
1986　Chris Van Allsburg, *The Polar Express*
1987　Richard Egielski, *Hey, Al* (text by Arthur Yorinks)
1988　C. John Schoenherr, *Owl Moon* (text by Jane Yolen)
1989　Stephen Gammell, *Song and Dance Man* (text by Karen Ackerman)
1990　Ed Young, *Lon Po Po: A Red-Riding Hood Story from China*
1991　David Macaulay, *Black and White*
1992　David Wiesner, *Tuesday*
1993　Emily Arnold McCully, *Mirette on the High Wire*
1994　Alley Say, *Grandfather's Journey*
1995　David Diaz, *Smoky Night* (text by Eve Bunting)
1996　Peggy Rathmann, *Officer Buckle and Gloria*

Activity 15

SHE WROTE MURDER??

You become the investigator in this exercise. Research a murder case that has gone or is going to trial and decide it for yourself.

Was the accused found guilty of murder? Do you agree with the verdict? If not, explain your reasons. If so, was the punishment a just one? What are the implications to society for such a crime?

Describe the case in a research paper and answer the questions.

A list of cases that occurred from 1986 to 1993 are given to help you.

(Accused) Murderer(s)	Victims
Ellie Nesler	The man accused of molesting her son was killed
Frederic Tokars	Allegedly arranged the death of his wife Sara
Detroit Officers: Walter Budzyn and Larry Nerers	Beat a motorist who later died
Suicide or military murder	Sailor Allen Schindler
FBI Agent Mark Putnam	Susan Smith, lover/informant
Charles Stuart	Wife Carol
Carolyn Warmus	Lover's wife, Betty Jeanne, was murdered
Richard Crafts (Woodchipper Murder)	Wife Helle Crafts
Robert Bardo (stalker)	Actress Rebecca Schaeffer
Joseph Fredericks	Christopher Stephenson, an 11 year old, was raped and killed
Cult leader Roch Theriault	2 murdered; over 25 "damaged"
Pamela Smart (school advisor)	Allegedly seduced a teenager to kill her husband
David & Ginger Twitchell	2 year old son died due to lack of medical care (Christian Scientists)

Jose & Erik Menendez	Sons accused of murdering parents, Jose & Kitty, who allegedly sexually molested boys
Lawrencia "Bambi" Bembenek	Husband's ex-wife Christine Schultz
Michael Griffin	Dr. Gunn, abortion doctor
Jean Harris	Received clemency for Scarsdale Diet murder
Olivia Riner, nanny	3 month old Kristie Fischer
Shannon & Melissa Garrison	Mother who was too strict
Jennifer Reali	Dainne Hood (believes only has to repent to make murder okay)

RESEARCH TOPICS OF HISTORICAL INTERNATIONAL CRIMES

The Madeline Smith Case   1857
The Prolific Thomas Neill Cream   1878–1892
The Peltzer Case   1882
The Whitechapel Murders   1888
The Lizzie Borden Case   1892
The Hawley Harvey Crippen Case   1910
The Henri Désiré Landru, Blubeard   1914–1919
The Snyder-Gray Case   1927
The Enigmatic Wallace Murder   1931
The De Koven Case   1937
The Brooke-Heath Killings   1946

Supreme Court Cases

Selected Reference Books
Any general encyclopedia
Constitutional Law Dictionary
Encyclopedia of the American Constitution
Encyclopedia of the American Judicial System
Guide to American Law
Guide to the U.S. Supreme Court
Magill's History of North America
Shepard's United States Supreme Court Case Names Citator
Supreme Court Reporter

Databases — Resources (see pages 101–143)
INFOTRAC (Legal-Information Access)

The following search engines can find available web sites:

Alta Vista	http://altavista.digital.com
Excite	http://www.excite.com
Open Text	http://www.opentext.com.8080
Inktomi	http://inktomi.berkeley.edu/query.html

The Elements of a Legal Citation

Here is an example of legal citation and a description of its parts.

Roe v. Wade, 410 U.S. 113, 93 S.Ct. 705 (1973)

Descriptions:

Roe v. Wade	Name of case
410	Volume number
U.S.	United States reports
113	Page on which case begins
93	Volume number
S.Ct.	Supreme Court reporter
705	Page number
(1973)	Year case was decided

When you need the full text of a state's statutes, legislation, constitution, or session laws, check "Full-text state statutes and legislation on the Internet," now located at:

http://www.prairienet.org/

Activity 16

SUPREME COURT CASES
JUDGING THE WORDS WE LIVE BY

Choose a case to investigate from the list below or find one on your own. After researching the case, decide if you agree or disagree with the Supreme Court's decision and why.

Supreme Court Case	Main Issue
Georgia v. McCollum (1992)	Elimination of prospective jurors on the basis of race/sex
R.A.B. v. St. Paul (1992)	Hate crime ordinance
Osborne v. Ohio (1990)	Child pornography
Idaho v. Wright (1990)	Hearsay evidence
Michigan Dept. of State Police v. Sitz (1990)	Sobriety checkpoints
Burnley v. Railway Labor Executives (1989) and *National Treasury Employees Union v. Von Raab*	Drug testing of employees
Florida Star *v. B.J.F.* (1989)	Privacy — Publishing victims' I.D.
Florida v. Riley (1989)	Helicopter surveillance
Penry v. Lynaugh (1989)	Death for mentally retarded murderer
Wilkins v. Missouri (decided by *Stanford v. Kentucky*) (1989)	Execution of kids convicted of murder

Hustler *v. Jerry Falwell*	Libel
Greenwood v. California (1988)	Garbage searches
Hazelwood School District v. Kuhlmeier (1988)	School newspapers and the 1st Amendment
Texas v. Johnson (1988)	Flag burning
McClesky v. Kemp (1987)	GA death penalty racist
Mozert v. Hawkins County Board of Education (1987)	Religion and public schools
Moran v. Burbine (1986)	Waiving of Miranda rights
Press-Enterprise Co. v. Superior Ct. (1986)	Free press
Bowers v. Hardwick (1986)	Homosexuals and privacy
United States v. Whaley (1986)	Good faith searches
Goldman v. Weinberger (1986)	Religious clothing and the military
Baston v. Kentucky (1986)	Impartial jury
Anderson v. Liberty Lobby (1986)	Libel: establishing malice
Wallace v. Jaffre (1985)	School prayer
United States v. Leon (1985)	Exclusionary rule
Silkwood v. Kerr-McGee Corporation (1984)	Federalism: nuclear power plants
Lynch v. Donnelly (1984)	Religious freedom: creches
Pyler v. Doe (1982)	Aliens: right to public education
United States v. Ross (1982)	Automobile searches
Dames and Moore v. Regan (1981)	Presidency: Iran Hostage Crisis
Rostker v. Goldberg (1981)	Sexual equality and the draft
Vance v. Terrazas (1980)	Aliens: establishing citizenship
Carey v. Brown (1980)	Labor: right to peaceful demonstration
Committee for Public Education and Religious Liberty v. Regan (1980)	Freedom of religion and state money

Fullilove v. Klutznick (1980)	Discrimination: the minority business enterprise requirements
Diamond v. Chakrabarty (1980)	Congressional powers and patents
Snepp v. United States (1980)	Contracts: publishing CIA information
Williams and Diamond v. Zbaraz (1980) and *Harris v. McRaie* (1980)	Funding of abortion
First National Bank of Boston v. Bellotti (1978)	Commercial speech
Hicklin v. Orbeck (1978)	Federalism: Alaska Hire Act
Stump v. Sparkman (1978)	Court jurisdiction: mother orders daughter sterilized
Bakke v. The University of California (1978)	Affirmative action
Goss v. Lopez (1975)	Due process: school suspension
O'Connor v. Donaldson (1975)	State mental hospital patients
Milliken v. Bradley (1974)	Bussing
United States v. Nixon (1974)	Presidential powers
Gertz v. Welch (1974)	Libel
Roe v. Wade (1973)	Abortion
Paris Adult Theater v. Slaton (1973)	Pornography
Frontiero v. Richardson (1973)	Sex discrimination
Sierra Club v. Morton (1972) also *Kleppe v. Sierra* (1976)	Environmental rights and national parks
Coolidge v. New Hampshire (1971)	Plain view doctrine
New York Times *v. United States* (1971)	Pentagon papers
Oregon v. Mitchell (1970)	Voting rights
Miranda v. Arizona (1966)	Right to remain silent
Gideo v. Wainwright (1963)	Due process

Hear Ye! Hear Ye!

THE 4TH AMENDMENT AND
HIGH TECHNOLOGY CASES

United States v. Knotts (1983)   Police surveillance

United States v. Torres (1984)   FBI surveillance

Rhode Island v. Delaurier (1985)   Cordless telephones

Florida v. Riley (1989)   Helicopter surveillance

INFOTRAC— Legal-Information Access

Activity 17

RESEARCHING A WORD

Choose a word that is used in Shakespearean works. Avoid words like "love" or "hate." Use as many CD-ROM and multimedia sources that are available.

1. Look up your word in a CD-ROM dictionary. Copy the word's etymology and its first definition. _____

_____

_____

2. Look up your word in a CD-ROM thesaurus. Copy the first synonyms. _____

_____

_____

3. Look up the word in a Bible. Copy a verse which contains your word.

_____

_____

_____

4. Look up your word in a book of quotations. Copy a quotation in which your word appears. _____

_____

_____

5. Look up your word in *INFOTRAC*. Find a full text article from a magazine dealing with your word. Summarize the article. _____

_____

_____

6. Look up your word in *Oxford English Dictionary*. Copy the first paragraph for your word. _____

_____

_____

Writing the Paper

This paper is as much about the process of discovering your word as it is about your word itself. Write the most interesting bit of information you discovered about your word. How has the word changed throughout history? Does it have a similar meaning today as compared to biblical times?

Bibliography

Follow an appropriate format or MLA for works cited page.

Shakespeare Glossary

all-thing wholly
an't if it
auger-hole tiny spot
augures prophecies
bechanc'd happened
beholding indebted
benison blessing
betimes quickly
blow our nails together wait patiently
bodements omens
bootless in vain
breech'd covered
brindl'd spotted
broad words speaking freely
brooch'd adorned
bruited reported
buzzard worthless person
chare chore
check rebuke
clept called
closet room
cloudy sullen
coign corner
complexion disposition
conceit thought
corporal agent muscle
counters coins
coz cousin; relative
cozen cheat
daff't doff it; take it off
dearest chuck term of endearment
ducat gold coin
dudgeon dagger hilt
enow enough
estate social position; condition
ewer jug
eyne eyes
fain willingly
father old man
fay faith
fil'd defiled

firstling first
foison plenty
forebear leave
free hearts true feelings
full of lead in low spirits
ghosted haunted
God 'ild us God reward us
golden round crown
graff graft
graymalkin gray cat
groom servant
habiliments attire
half a soul halfwit
hand handwriting
haply per chance
hart male deer
hilding nasty beast or wretch
hind deer
hipp'd lame
ho halt
hurlyburly tumult
I'll do do him harm
in a few briefly
in compt brought to account
incarnadine turn red
insane root hemlock
is't call'd is it
Jack name used in contempt; servant; drinking utensil
jade tired horse
Jill maid; drinking utensil
keep counsel keep a secret
lank'd thin
lethe death
levell'd at guessed
loose let go
lover friend
make boot take advantage
make to approach
maw and gulf gullet and stomach
meed reward
meetly pretty good

mew her up confine her
milch-kine milking cows
moe more
moiety part
mortified deadened
napkins handkerchiefs
nave to the chops navel to the throat
near'st of life vital organs
noddle head
outface it bluff it out
ow'd owned
owe own
paddock toad
parlous dangerous
patch fool
poke pocket
posts messengers
prime spring
priser prizefighter
proper handsome
raise the waters start things moving
rate scold; rebuke
roundly directly
roynish mangy
rudesby rough young man
scanted limited
scape escape
scarf up blindfold
seated in the mean living comfortably
second cock 3:00 A.M.
signs well good omen
sith since
skirr scour
sooth true
spaniel'd me followed me
speak me fair speak well of me
spoiled plundered
spot blemish
stay keep
stay'd her let her stay

Activity 18

AUTHORS' FAMOUS LAST WORDS

Students can research famous authors in the electronic encyclopedias, *Gale's Discovering Authors,* or other multimedia programs about authors which is available in the library. The students may choose any of the following famous last words of famous authors and write an obituary of the famous author. They could use the local or national newspapers obituary page to get an idea about how to write an obituary. They may write these obituaries for the school news which many schools now televise on school video news programs via channel 1 or they could create their own news programs and make a multimedia presentation. The students will use many communication skills as they work in cooperative learning groups to research, write, and produce.

Databases:
1. *Bartlett's Familiar Quotations*
2. *Current Biography on CD*
3. *Gale's Discovering Authors*

FAMOUS PEOPLE

Elizabeth Barrett Browning	Cotton Mather
Robert Browning	Sir Thomas Moore
Lord Byron	Edgar Allan Poe
Hart Crane	George Bernard Shaw
Benjamin Franklin	Robert Louis Stevenson
Alfred Houseman	Henry David Thoreau
Washington Irving	Walt Whitman
John Keats	Oscar Wilde

Authors' Famous Last Words

"Knowledge by suffering entereth, And life is perfected by death."—*Elizabeth Barrett Browning*

"How gratifying!"—*Robert Browning*

"The damned doctors have drenched me so that I can scarcely stand. I want to sleep now."—*Lord Byron*

"Goodbye, everybody!"—*Hart Crane (as he jumped overboard)*

"A dying man can do nothing easy."—*Benjamin Franklin*

"I am about the extent of a tenth of a gnat's eyebrow better."—*Joel Chandler Harris*

"Yes, that's a good one, and tomorrow I shall be telling it again on the Golden Floor."—*Alfred Houseman*

"Well, I must arrange my pillows for another weary night! When will this end?"—*Washington Irving*

"Lift me up for I am dying. I shall die easy. Don't be frightened. Thank God it has come."—*John Keats*

"Is this dying? Is this all? Is this what I feared when I prayed against a hard death? Oh, I can bear this! I can bear it!"—*Cotton Mather*

"Pluck up thy spirits, man, and be not afraid to do thine office: My neck is very short; take heed, therefore, thou strike not awry, for saving of thine honesty."—*Sir Thomas More (to his executioner)*

"Lord, help my poor soul."—*Edgar Allan Poe*

"Sister, you're trying to keep me alive as an old curiosity, but I'm done, I'm finished, I'm going to die."—*George Bernard Shaw*

"My head, my head!"—*Robert Louis Stevenson*

"Moose, Indian."—*Henry David Thoreau*

"Garrulous to the very last."—*Walt Whitman*

"I'm dying as I've lived: beyond my means; this wallpaper is killing me; one of us has got to go."—*Oscar Wilde*

Activity 19

Social Studies

Goals: To assist students in becoming actual investigators of real global
   problems.
   To provide students with opportunities for taking an active part
   in formulating problems to be investigated.
   To assist students with electronic data.
   To provide students with an opportunity to apply critical thinking skills to global problems.

Steps in the research process:
   1. Select the topic
   2. Define the topic
   3. Ask questions about the topic
   4. Select the key words or main terms
   5. Gather information about topic
   6. Organize information
   7. Analyze information
   8. Utilize information

Topic: _____

Problem: You have been selected to become a participate in the United
   Nations Global Environmental conference. You and the members of
   your team will represent the country and citizens of _____.
   All countries on the planet are interdependent upon each other, sharing the same successes and problems. Diseases in Africa, oil spills in
   Saudi Arabia, and acid rain in Canada have an effect on each continent. Your task is to search and analyze information about the environmental problems and policies of your country. Consider the location, human resources, culture, health, history, and education of your
   country. Predict how the environmental problems of this country can
   affect the United States.

Terms and key words: _____

_____

_____

Questions about topic: _____

_____

_____

List the databases and multimedia programs you used to find information:

_____

_____

_____

Suggested multimedia resources (pages 101–143):
1. *Countries of the World Encyclopedias*
2. *Countries of the World*

Geography sites:
Aurora Borealis: The Northern Lights   http://www.uit.no/npt/nordlyset/waynorth/00-innhold.en.html

Bamboo Forests and Panda Conservation in China   http://www.gis.psu.edu/Taylor/TaylorHTML/TaylorPanda.html

C&C's Earth Science Emporium   http://nlu.nl.edu/bthu/nlu/eight/es/Homepage.html

Environmental Education Resources   http://envirolink.org/enviroed/students.html

The Geographer's Craft Project   http://www.utexas.edu/depts/grg/gcraft/contents.html

Introduction to Glaciers   http://www.whistler.net/glacier/index.html

Land Surveying   http://userzweb.lightspeed.net/~rolsen/survey.htm

Population Ecology Home Page   http://www.gypsymoth.ento.vt.edu/~sharov/popechome/welcome.html

Remote Sensing Series   http://www.geo.unizh.ch/rs12/remote_sensing_series/

Statistical Abstract: U.S. Statistics   http://www.census.gov/stat_abstract/

This Human World: An Introduction to Geography   http://www.utexas.edu/depts/grg/virtdept/samples/english/english.html

Understanding Our Planet Through Chemistry   http://helios.cr.usgs.gov/gips/aii-home.htm

Activity 20

MULTIMEDIA BOOK/MOVIE REVIEW

Name _____

Choose a movie which you have seen on the screen and complete the following information about your film.

Name of movie: _____

Director: _____

Go to the *INFOTRAC Periodical Index* or another periodical index with abstracts or full text. Choose a movie review of your movie and summarize the review. _____

_____

Author/reviewer: _____

Write a critical review of your movie and compare your review with the professional review you researched. The length of the review should be no less than one page. _____

_____

_____

Read a book which is based on the movie. Research a review from a periodical index or the *New York Times* CD-ROM database. Summarize the review and write your own review as you did with the movie review.

Title of book: _____

Author of book: _____

Author/reviewer: _____

Write a contrast/comparison paper contrasting the movie with the book.

Suggested multimedia resources:
1. *INFOTRAC–CD-ROM*
2. *New York Times–CD-ROM*
3. *Movie Select–CD-ROM*
4. *Books in Print with Book Reviews Plus/Europe*

Suggested Lists of Books That Have Become Movies

Author	Title
Robin Cook	*Coma*
Roald Dahl	*Witches*
John Farris	*The Fury*
Arthur Clark	*2001: A Space Odyssey*
Isaac Asimov	*The Fantastic Voyage*
Stephen King	*The Running Man* (Bachman)
Frank Herbert	*Dune*
Andre Norton	*The Beast Master*
Michael Crichton	*Jurassic Park*
Issac Asimov	*Foundation*
Ursula Le Guin	*The Dispossessed*
Robert Heinlein	*Friday*
C.S. Lewis	*Out of the Silent Planet*
William Shakespeare	*Hamlet*
H.G. Wells	*The War of the Worlds*
John Grisham	*The Firm*
Louisa M. Alcott	*Little Women*
Alice Walker	*The Color Purple*
Toni Morrison	*Beloved*
Jane Austen	*Emma*

Activity 21

WONDER?

Find as many answers as possible using the multimedia resources. Work in cooperative learning groups or individually.

Wonder:

What lives in ponds?
Why do some animals hibernate?
Why do rabbits have big ears?
How are fossils formed?
Do pine cones have a purpose?
How do fish breathe?
Why do beavers build dams?
How do snakes crawl out of their skins?
How fast can animals go?
How do bats navigate?
How do animals make tracks?
How do bees make honey?
What is a snowflake?
How do tree frogs climb?
How long can camels go without water?
What bird picks the teeth of crocodiles?

Multimedia resources:

1. *Great Wonders of the World, Vol. I*
2. *Great Wonders of the World, Vol. II*
3. *Compton's Interactive Encyclopedia*
4. *All About Science*
5. *Multimedia Audubon's Mammals*

Activity 22

INTERNET

The resources below can be found on the World Wide Web using a program called "Lynx."

To get Lynx access to the World Wide Web, go to the $.

Type "LYNX"

Press return

Follow the directions

At the $, type URL or HTTP addresses

To get to Thomas, go to $

Type: LYNX HTTP://THOMAS.LOC.GOV.

You will get the home page of Thomas, the World Wide Web server administered by the Library of Congress. This is a government database.

OR USE SEARCH ENGINES

1. *Yahoo!*
http://www.yahoo.com
     A directory of the Internet arranged by categories, this can be your gateway to many other sites online.

2. *AltaVista*
http://www.altavista.digital.com
     Another helpful information finder, AltaVista lets you locate sites and documents with its powerful search feature. Type in a few key words (e.g., *Olympics* and *Sydney*) and up pop links to relevant pages giving details about the 2000 games.

Activity 23

REFERENCE
WORLD ALMANACS AND CD-ROM RESOURCES

Almanacs and factual resources provide statistical and current information on a wide range of subjects.

Directions
Find an almanac or CD-ROM resource and answer the following questions.

1. Who was the twenty-first president of the United States? _____

_____

2. What is the population of the United States? _____

3. Who is the leader of Pakistan? _____

4. Name the largest body of water in the world. _____

_____

5. Under the topic "government officials," who would become president if the president and vice president of the United States were assassinated?

_____

6. How many people died during the major California earthquakes?

		Richter Scale	*Deaths*
1906	San Francisco	8.3	_____
1923	North Coast	7.2	_____
1989	San Francisco	7.0	_____

Multimedia Resources
1. *Multimedia World Fact Book and CIA World Tour*
2. *CIA World Fact Book*
3. *Compton's Interactive Encyclopedia*

Resources

About Cows. *Producer:* Quanta Press. *Operating System:* PC/MAC. *Subject:* Science. *Price:* $29. *Grade Level:* General. *Hardware:* IBM PC, XT, AT, or compatible; CD-ROM player with card and cable; printer for text (optional). *Software:* PC-DOS or MS-DOS 2.1 or higher, Microsoft CD-ROM extensions. *Distributor:* CDiscovery.

This CD-ROM is a reprint of the Northwood Press volume *About Cows* by Sara Rath. It contains a full text database on one of nature's most wonderful beasts plus black and white and color images of various bovine poses. The disk is for both amateur and serious bovinologists alike.

Academic Abstracts (AA) Full Text Elite — Academic. *Producer:* EBSCO Publishing. *Operating System:* PC. *Subject:* Reference. *Price:* $4,499. *Grade Level:* JH, HS, C. *Hardware:* IBM PC, XT compatible 640K RAM; one double-sided drive; 5MB hard disk space available. *Software:* PC-DOS or MS-DOS 3.2 or higher; Microsoft CD-ROM extensions version 2.10. *Distributor:* EBSCO.

Academic Abstracts (AA) Full Text Elite combines key word access to abstracts or articles from 747 general interest magazines plus the *New York Times*, with key word access to full text magazine articles. Full text for 30 reference magazines, including *Newsweek, The Economist*, and *Congressional Quarterly*, is included. Also includes thousands of Magill Book Reviews by Salem Press in full text.

Aesop's Fables. Ebook Inc., 32970 Alvarado-Niles Road, Suite 704, Union City, CA 94587; 510/429-1331. *Fax:* 510/429-1394. *Tech. Support:* 510/713-8904. *Price:* $29.95. *Platform:* MPC. *Grade level:* Primary, Elementary. *Curriculum:* Storybook.

Aesop's wise and witty tales told through an interactive story program. Includes narration and graphics.

Aesop's Fables. *Operating System:* DOS, MAC. *Subject:* Children's Literature. *Grade Level:* General. *Hardware:* DOS 5.0; IBM 386, 2MB RAM, VGA monitor, audio card, mouse; Macintosh, 1MB RAM. *Software:* Windows 3.x compatible, Macintosh System 6.0.5. *Distributor:* Updata.

Discover the world of reading in this interactive medium where Aesop's tales are presented with original text and new illustrations. Narration, music and sound effects guide the reader through the stories. Click on any word or picture to obtain pronunciation syllables or an in-context explanation of any word. Hear a single sentence or the entire disk. Titles include: *The Crab and His Mother, The Fox and the Grapes, The Ants and the Grasshopper.*

Aesop's Multimedia Fables. *Operating System:* MPC. *Subject:* Children's Literature. *Grade Level:* General. *Hardware:* See distributor. *Software:* See distributor. *Distributor:* Updata.
    Includes all 54 of Aesop's fables with illustrations by Sir Arthur Rackham and narration by Mary and Virginia Fielder. Contains on-screen dictionary.

African American Experience. Globe Fearon Educational Publisher, P.O. Box 2649, Columbus, OH 43216; 800/848-9500. *Fax:* 614/771-7361. *Price:* $99, school. *Platform:* Macintosh, DOS. *Grade Level:* HS.*Curriculum:* Social Studies.
    An electronic textbook that tells the history of African Americans beginning in the African homeland. Includes the African continent explorers, freedom fighters, politics, biographies, culture and social life.

The African American Experience: A History. *Operating System:* DOS. *Subject:* African American History. *Grade Level:* JH, HS, C. *Hardware:* IBM PC, 640K RAM, VGA monitor. *Software:* DOS 3.1. *Distributor:* Updata.
    Traces the history of African Americans, beginning in the African homeland. Topics include: the African continent, explorers, freedom fighters, biographies, culture, and social life.

African American History. *Operation System:* DOS, MAC. *Subject:* African American History. *Grade Level:* General. *Hardware:* See distributor. *Software:* See distributor. *Distributor:* Updata.
    A multimedia program covering the slave trade and conditions of slavery, the Civil War, the Harlem Renaissance, the depression, equal rights, segregation, and more. Illustrations and narration from 75 personalities including Sojourner Truth, Booker T. Washington, A. Philip Randolph, James Baldwin, and others.

All About Science. *Producer:* Intellectual Software. *Operating System:* MAC. *Subject:* Science. *Price:* $395. *Grade Level:* Elem., JH, HS. *Hardware:* See distributor. *Distributor:* CDiscovery.
    Collection of 48 interactive programs that cover all elementary through intermediate science topics in a high-interest format. The programs include: Elementary Science II — electricity, elementary physics, elementary chemistry, elementary biology I & II, behavioral sciences; Investigating Our World package — earth and moon system, minerals, rock, solar system, stars and galaxies, weather and climate, and weather and erosion; Investigating Matter and Energy package — classifying elements, compounds, heat, how matter changes magnets and electromagnetism, metric system, MMV electricity, MMV force and motion, physical science, properties of matter, and work and machines; Science of Living Things package — describing how living things are alike, describing patterns reproduction, discovering how animals stay alive, discovering how plants grow, following genetics from generation to generation, organizing all natural things, organizing animals, organizing plants, organizing protists and fungi, tracing cycle in the environment; ecology, tracking changes through time: evolution, and understanding the human fight to stay healthy, and understanding systems of the human body.

Allie's Playhouse. Opcode Systems Inc., 3950 Fabian Way, Suite 100, Palo Alto, CA 94303; 800/557-2633 (orders); 415/856-3333. *Fax:* 415/494-1113. *Tech. Support:*

415/494-9393. *Price:* $59.95. *Platform:* Macintosh, MPC. *Grade Level:* Primary. *Curriculum:* Storybook.

An interactive educational program to encourage children to explore and experiment, make decisions, take risks, make mistakes, succeed and, most importantly, learn.

American Civil War: A Nation Divided. *Operating System:* Windows. *Subject:* History. *Grade Level:* General. *Hardware:* IBM 386, 4MB RAM, hard disk, VGA monitor, mouse. *Software:* Windows 3.1. *Distributor:* Updata.

Search the database by date, name, event, invasion, anecdote, and more. Gain instant access to over 1,200 dramatic photographs and 100 maps. Play video clips of realistic reenactments, and access war stories and anecdotes.

American Heritage: Illustrated Encyclopedia Dictionary. XIPHIAS, 8758 Venice Boulevard, Los Angeles, CA 90034; 800/421-9194 (sales); 310/841-2790. *Fax:* 310/841-2559. *Price:* $39.95. *Platform:* DOS, MPC. *Grade Level:* HS. *Curriculum:* Reference and Interdisciplinary.

A multimedia reference of over 180,000 definitions and thousands of colorful pictures, with the ability to look up words without knowing the spelling or by the use of a hot word to call up all definitions associated with the word.

The American Heritage Talking Dictionary. *Operating System:* MAC, Windows. *Subject:* Reference. *Grade Level:* General. *Hardware:* See distributor. *Software:* See distributor. *Distributor:* Updata.

More than 200,000 words, including their complete definitions, parts of speech, proper usage, hyphenation, idioms, synonyms, homographs, and abbreviations. Each word is pronounced by a trained linguist. Also includes *Roget's Electronic Thesaurus* with 500,000 synonyms. Allows users to locate words with bits of definition and parts of spellings. Includes biographical, geographical, and college information.

The American Indian: A Multimedia Encyclopedia. Facts on File, Inc., 460 Park Avenue South, New York, NY 10016-7382; 800/322-8755; 212/683-2244. *Fax:* 212/683-3633. *Tech. Support:* 800/322-8755. *Price:* $295. *Platform:* DOS. *Grade Level:* HS. *Curriculum:* Social Studies.

A complete and comprehensive source of information on the native peoples of the North American continent; includes full text of rare documents and treaties from the National Archives, 1,100 images and sound bites of authentic American Indian songs and colorful stories and legends.

The American Indian: A Multimedia Encyclopedia. *Operating System:* DOS. *Subject:* Native American History and Culture. *Grade Level:* JH to Adult. *Hardware:* See distributor. *Software:* See distributor. *Distributor:* Updata.

Provides access to thousands of historical treasures on over 450 North American Indian tribes, including rare maps, documents, photos, illustrations, sound bites and biographical entries. Features the complete text of: *Voices of the Winds, Atlas of the American Indian, Who Was Who in Native American History*, and *Encyclopedia of Native American Tribes*. Includes over 1,100 VGA illustrations, including original photos, etc. Also contains recorded sounds of authentic American Indian songs. Topics

Animal Alphabet. REMedia, Inc., 13525 Midland Road, Poway, CA 92064; 619/486-5030. *Tech. Support:* 619/486-5030. *Price:* $39.95. *Platform:* Macintosh. *Grade Level:* Primary. *Curriculum:* Language Arts.

Each letter in the alphabet is represented by an animal cartoon with a page of spoken text and a video sequence.

Animal Kingdom. *Operating System:* DOS, MAC, MPC. *Subject:* Stock photography. *Grade Level:* General. *Hardware:* See distributor. *Software:* See distributor. *Distributor:* Updata.

Explores nature from the Savannah to the tundra through 25 action videos, 100 audio clips and 100 dynamic images. The self-running slide show and accompanying search software make the clips easy and fun to view and use.

Animal Tales. *Operating System:* MAC, MPC. *Subject:* Early Reading. *Grade Level:* K–1. *Hardware:* See distributor. *Software:* See distributor. *Distributor:* Updata.

A series of six stories that takes early readers on original journeys addressing such tough moral issues as self-acceptance, respect and fear. Includes six paperback books.

Annabel's Dream of Ancient Egypt. *Operating System:* PC/MAC. *Subject:* Reading/Music/Egypt. *Price:* $69. *Grade Level:* Elem. *Hardware:* IBM PC, 640 RAM, DOS; Macintosh. *Distributor:* Updata.

An original children's story about a cat who dreams of being a queen. The story is fully illustrated and narrated in stereo CD-audio with built-in story controls designed to build stronger reading skills. These include a multimedia glossary, spelling, games, and more. Learning topics such as ancient Egypt and opera are introduced in separate modules complete with images, audio, story and music selections. In addition, there are many hands-on activities like a hieroglyphics translator, a recipe for making paper, an excavation exercise, portrait gallery, and more. Assembled by well-known children's reference author Alan Carpenter and written by Jere Williams.

Aquatic Sciences and Fisheries Abstracts. *Producer:* Cambridge Scientific Abstracts. *Operating System:* PC. *Subject:* Science. *Price:* $2,495. *Grade Level:* JH, HS, C. *Hardware:* IBM PC or compatible; 640K RAM; standard CD-ROM player. *Software:* PC-DOS or MS-DOS 2.1 or higher. *Distributor:* EBSCO.

A complete international database containing entries drawn from literature supplied by the United Nations Department of International Economic Aid and Social Affairs (FAO), the Intergovernmental Oceanographic Commission (IOC), and leading research centers throughout the world. Included are abstracts and citations from leading journals, as well as reports, serial monographs, dissertations, covering all biological and ecological aspects of marine, freshwater, and brackish environments.

Archives of History. *Operating System:* MAC, MPC. *Subject:* 20th Century History. *Grade Level:* General. *Hardware:* See distributor. *Software:* See distributor. *Distributor:* Updata.

Contains more than 250 QuickTime movies of the most dramatic and profound events of the 20th century. Includes rare footage from the World Wars; images of Ghandi, Trotsky, Kennedy and King; video of floods, famines and disasters; and a sweeping survey of historical fads and lifestyles.

Arctic and Antarctic Regions (1959–Present). *Producer:* National Information Services Corporation. *Operating System:* PC. *Subject:* Science. *Price:* $811. *Grade Level:* General. *Hardware:* IBM PC, XT, AT, PS/2 or compatible; 512 RAM; any CD-ROM drive; monochrome or color monitor. *Software:* PC-DOS or MS-DOS, Microsoft CD-ROM extensions. *Distributor:* EBSCO.

Contains citations compiled by the Science and Technology Division of the U.S. Library of Congress. Five new databases have recently been added: ASTIS, C-CORE, CITATION, SPRILIB, AORIS. All 40 years of the database are indexed on one CD-ROM. The database covers aspects of the life, physical and social sciences, and related engineering, biology, ozone and other matters.

Astrology Source. *Operating System:* MAC, MPC. *Subject:* Astronomy. *Grade Level:* JH to Adult. *Hardware:* See distributor. *Software:* See distributor. *Distributor:* Updata.

Narrated tutorials explain astrological influences. Create and print customized astrological and compatibility charts. Contains easy to use daily horoscope and natal charts. Also includes a full index and glossary.

Astronomer-CD. *Operating System:* Windows. *Subject:* Astronomy. *Grade Level:* JH to Adult. *Hardware:* See distributor. *Software:* See distributor. *Distributor:* Updata.

Examine 11,000 stars, planets, galaxies, comets, nebulae and constellations via 400 pictures, 40 minutes of color video, and 300 text articles. Users learn about and experience Neil Armstrong's first steps on the moon. All articles are written in layman's terms and charts can be printed.

Atlas of U.S. Presidents. *Operating System:* MAC, MPC. *Subject:* General reference, U.S. Presidents. *Grade Level:* General. *Hardware:* See distributor. *Software:* See distributor. *Distributor:* Updata.

Portraits, searchable facts and biographies of each of the first 41 presidents of the United States. Also includes summaries of election results and portraits and biographies of each first lady.

Audio Notes. *Producer:* Warner. *Operating System:* MAC. *Subject:* Music. *Price:* $66 each. *Grade Level:* HS. *Hardware:* At least 1 meg of RAM and hard disk drive with 6.5 MB of free space. *Software:* See distributor. *Distributor:* CDiscovery.

A new CD collection combining digital musical performances with text, pictures, and audio in an environment presentation controlled by the listener. Conducted by Robert Shaw, "A German Requiem" is performed in this two-disk set (including Hypercard 2.0) and enhanced by pictures, commentaries, additional music, analysis, historical information, musical glossary and index, all interactively accessible by a MAC. Features include the Harmonic Plan to explore how Brahms used harmony, instant access to any part of the music, including all the themes and their transformations. Fifty side journeys enhance the musical experience with richly illustrated biographical, historical, and musical insights.

Audubon's Mammals. *Operating System:* PC/MAC. *Subject:* Science. *Price:* $158 Net; $79 References; *Grade Level:* General. *Hardware:* See distributor. *Software:* See distributor. *Distributor:* CDiscovery.

John James Audubon's 1840 edition of *Quadrupeds of North America* in full color, text and CD quality sounds from Cornell University's Library of Natural Sounds for many of the mammals.

Barron's Book Notes. *Operating System:* DOS, Windows. *Subject:* Literature. *Grade Level:* JH to Adult. *Hardware:* See distributor. *Software:* See distributor. *Distributor:* Updata.

Contains 101 book notes from classic literary works featuring illustrations, critical analysis of works, study guides, and sample tests. Search of era, age, century, region, country or subject.

Barron's Complete Book Notes. World Library Inc., 2809 Main Street, Irvine, CA 92714; 800/443-0238; 714/756-9500. *Fax:* 714/756-9511. *Tech. Support:* 714/756-9550. *Price:* $89. *Platform:* Macintosh, DOS, Windows. *Grade Level:* HS. *Curriculum:* Language Arts.

Complete unabridged text of 101 literary guides including plot summaries, discussions, analyses and author biographies.

Barron's Profiles of American Colleges. *Operating System:* DOS, MAC, MPC. *Subject:* College Reference Guide. *Grade Level:* JH to Adult. *Hardware:* See distributor. *Software:* See distributor. *Distributor:* Updata.

Covers 1,500 colleges nationwide. Includes full color maps of each state for geographic location of all schools and an hour of video. Search for colleges by state, tuition range and subject major.

Bartlett's Familiar Quotations *(multimedia).* Expanded Multimedia Edition. CD-ROM. *Platform:* Macintosh, Windows. *Hardware:* See distributor. *Software:* See distributor. *Distributor:* Tim Warner. *Price:* $39.95.

This CD-ROM multimedia edition includes the entire 16th edition of the famous quotation source with added sound files, still art and video clips.

Baseball's Greatest Hits. Voyager, 1 Bridge Street, Irvington, NY 10533; 800/446-2001. *Fax:* 914/591-6481. *Tech. Support:* 914/591-5500. *Price:* $59.95. *Platform:* Macintosh. *Grade Level:* JH, HS. *Curriculum:* Sports.

Sixty-five of baseball's greatest moments with introductions by Mel Allen, the radio announcement of the actual event, and video clips when available. Hundreds of photos, player statistics, team histories and rosters; includes a baseball trivia game.

Beauty and the Beast. *Operating System:* MAC. *Subject:* Children's Literature. *Grade Level:* K–6. *Hardware:* See distributor. *Software:* See distributor. *Distributor:* Updata.

A brand-new version of the classic romance about love conquering all obstacles. Beautiful animation and illustrations are augmented by an extensive soundtrack.

Beauty and the Beast: A Multimedia Storybook. *Operating System:* MPC. *Subject:* Children's Fairy Tale. *Grade Level:* General. *Hardware:* See distributor. *Software:* See distributor. *Distributor:* Updata.

Has 60 minutes of narration, and original art in this multimedia storybook. Difficult words are highlighted and defined, and individual controls for story, pictures, and sound effects lead the way to a magical ending.

Beethoven Symphony #9. Voyager, 1 Bridge Street, Irvington, NY 10533; 800/446-2001. *Fax:* 914/591-6481. *Tech. Support:* 914/591-5500. *Price:* $99.95. *Platform:* Macintosh. *Grade Level:* HS. *Curriculum:* Arts and Music.

Five-part exploration of one of the world's greatest symphonies. Examines the musical score, individual instruments and the life and times of the composer.

Beethoven Symphony No. 9 CD Companion. *Producer:* Voyager. *Operating System:* PC/MAC. *Subject:* Music. *Price:* $78. *Grade Level:* HS, C. *Hardware:* Macintosh Plus, IBM 286, MS-DOS or MS-DOS 3.1. *Software:* Hypercard. *Distributor:* Updata.

An interactive disk that combines entertainment and education. The user can listen to Beethoven's magnificent Choral Symphony in whole or in part while choosing from a plethora of options. The user can choose moment by moment what he wants to do: listen while reading time-matched commentary by UCLA music professor Robert Winter, listen while viewing comments about the language of music or the life and times of Ludwig van Beethoven and more. During the vocal section of the Ninth Symphony's mighty finale, you can follow on screen the text of Schiller's "Ode to Joy," switching back and forth from English to German if you wish. You can play music passages that illustrate a particular concept, highlight words and press "Glossary," or play musical games. This can all be done while listening to the Ninth being performed by Hans Schmidt-Isserstedt conducting the Vienna State Opera and the Vienna Philharmonic.

Beethoven's 5th. *Operating System:* Windows. *Subject:* Music, Education. *Grade Level:* General. *Hardware:* See distributor. *Software:* See distributor. *Distributor:* Updata.

This musical voyage will inspire you to gain an understanding of classical music. Explore the inner workings of each movement by section, measure, and instrument, each accompanied by in-depth commentary.

The Best Literature Workbook Ever. *Operating System:* DOS, MAC. *Subject:* Foreign Language. *Grade Level:* General. *Hardware:* See distributor. *Software:* See distributor. *Distributor:* Updata.

A survey of literature covering: Short stories, Review of American Literature, Review of English Literature, Victoria Reading Comprehension designed to overcome problems in understanding passages containing new or unfamiliar words. Also has reproducible worksheets with over 1,000 printable pages for students and teachers.

Beyond the Wall of Stars. Creative Multimedia, 514 NW 11th Avenue, Suite 203, Portland, OR 97209; 800/262-7668; 503/241-4351. *Fax:* 503/241-4370. *Tech. Support:* 503/241-1530. *Price:* $49.99. *Platform:* Macintosh, MPC. *Grade Level:* JH, HS. *Curriculum:* Language Arts.

This grand quest, the first in a trilogy, leads you into a problem solving voyage of discovery that lets you direct the future to save planet Celadon through 3-D animation images, sound and text. You read, decide and solve your way through the Wall of Stars.

The Bible Library. *Producer:* Ellis Enterprises. *Operating System:* PC. *Subject:* Bible/Religion. *Price:* $149. *Grade Level:* HS, C, Adult. *Hardware:* IBM PC or compatible; 512K RAM; CD-ROM player; printer for text optional, monitor. *Software:* PC-DOS or MS-DOS, Microsoft CD-ROM extensions. *Distributor:* Bureau of Electronic Publishing.

Contains 9 Bibles and 20 reference works with 31 concordances of Bibles and their references. Strong's numbering system is linked to the original Bible languages. Contains 500 gospel sermons, 500 gospel illustrations, 2,000 miscellaneous short works. Quickly finds all occurrences of Hebrew, Greek, or English words. Five word studies, two dictionaries, two commentaries, and more. Comprehensive religious collection includes over 60 works. Nine complete Bibles: American Standard Version, Literal English Translation, King James Version, New King James Version, Simple English New Testament (four dictionaries and references), Easton's Bible Dictionary, Elwell's Evangelical Dictionary of the Theology, Living Bible, Romanized Hebrew-Greek Bible, New International Version, Revised Standard Version, Edersheim's Life and Times of Jesus the Messiah, Strong's Numbers Linked to Original Hebrew and Greek words. Six Sermon Outlines and Illustrations (3,000 sermons) consists of: 500 Basic Bible Truths, 500 Evangelistic Sermons, 500 Christian Life Sermons, 500 Children's Sermons, 500 Gospel Sermons, 500 Gospel Illustrations. Also provided are 2 Bible Language Dictionaries, 3 Word Studies, 2 Commentaries, and 101 Hymn Stories.

The Bible Library. *Operating System:* DOS. *Subject:* Religion. *Grade Level:* General. *Hardware:* See distributor. *Software:* See distributor. *Distributor:* Updata.

Combines 9 bibles and 20 reference works with 31 concordances of bibles and their references. Contains 2,500 gospel sermon outlines, 500 gospel illustrations, 2,000 miscellaneous short works.

Biography and Genealogy — Master Index. Gale Research Inc., 835 Penobscot Building, Detroit, MI 48226-4094; 800/877-GALE; 313/961-2242. *Fax:* 313/961-6083. *Tech. Support:* 800/877-4253, Ext. 6021. *Price:* $1,250. *Platform:* DOS. *Grade Level:* HS. *Curriculum:* Language Arts.

A comprehensive index to current and retrospective biographical dictionaries and who's who. Containing more than 8.8 million citations, provides access to more than 2,000 volumes and editions of over 675 biographical reference sources.

Biological Abstracts on Compact Disc. *Producer:* SilverPlatter Information. *Operating System:* PC. *Subject:* Science/Biomedical. *Price:* $8,325. *Grade Level:* JH, HS, C. *Hardware:* IBM PC or compatible; 640K RAM floppy or hard disk (hard disk recommended); CD-ROM player. *Software:* PC-DOS or MS-DOS 2.1 or higher, Microsoft CD-ROM extensions. *Distributor:* EBSCO.

The basic research tool for those in the biological and biomedical fields. Entries include bibliographic citations and abstracts of current research reported in biological and biomedical literature. Provides searchable information on authors' institutional affiliation, and language information for all citations. There are 250,000 records indexed per year.

Biology Digest on CD-ROM. NewsBank, Inc., 58 Pine Street, New Canaan, CT 06840-5426; 800/762-8182; 203/966-6254. *Fax:* 203/966-6254. *Tech. Support:* 800/762-8282. *Price:* $300, back files $600. *Platform:* DOS. *Grade Level:* HS. *Curriculum:* Science.

Extensive summaries of articles from over 170 scientific journals and science-related periodicals worldwide. Over 3,000 articles per year cover the areas of Viruses, Microflora and Plants, Animal Kingdom, Human Organism, Infectious Diseases, Population and Health, Cell Biology and Biogensis, Environment Quality, and Biology Education.

Birds of America. *Producer:* CMC ReSearch. *Operating System:* MAC/PC. *Subject:* Wildlife. *Price:* $99. *Grade Level:* JH, HS. *Hardware:* See distributor. *Software:* See distributor. *Distributor:* CDiscovery.

Bird calls can be played through headphones or external speakers. Multimedia disk contains the collection of the first edition plates (500 color VGA images) and text as well as 15 bird call recordings. Audubon describes each bird including its habitat and range. This disk offers high quality color illustrations, CD quality sound, and reference text.

Bodyworks, V3.0. *Operating System:* Windows. *Subject:* Physiology. *Grade Level:* JH to Adult. *Hardware:* See distributor. *Software:* See distributor. *Distributor:* Updata.

Discover the skeletal, muscular, cardiovascular, reproductive and other structures and systems which make up the body. Provides information on first aid, fitness, sports injuries, common illness, nutrition and more.

Book of Lists #3. *Operating System:* MAC, MPC. *Subject:* Trivia. *Grade Level:* General. *Hardware:* See distributor. *Software:* See distributor. *Distributor:* Updata.

This trivia disk contains thousands of incredible facts supported by drawings, pictures and sound. Includes descriptive information on a host of subjects including health, entertainment, politics, American history, etc.

Book of Lists #3. *Operating System:* PC/MAC. *Subject:* Reference. *Price:* $69.95. *Grade Level:* General. *Hardware:* See distributor. *Software:* See distributor. *Distributor:* New Media Source.

Trivia disk contains facts and information on a host of subjects including sports, sciences, space, entertainment, and more. Author David Wallechinsky makes sure learning through entertainment is fun.

Book Review Digest. *Producer:* H.W. Wilson. *Operating System:* PC. *Subject:* Reading. *Price:* $1,095. *Grade Level:* JH, HS, C. *Hardware:* IBM Personal System/2 series of computers or any IBM PC with 640K RAM; fixed disk drive or any WILSONLINE Workstation. *Software:* PC-DOS or MS-DOS, Microsoft CD-ROM extensions. *Distributor:* EBSCO.

Provides excerpts from and citations to reviews of current and adult fiction and nonfiction from *Book Review Digest.* Covers nearly 6,000 English-language books each year.

Books in Print Plus. Bowker Electronic Publishing, 121 Chanlon Road, New Providence, NJ 07974-1154; 800/323-3288. *Price:* By subscription. *Platform:* Macintosh. *Grade Level:* HS. *Curriculum:* Reference and Interdisciplinary.

Bibliographic information on all books currently published in the United States. Searchable by title, author, ISBN, publisher, grade level and keyword.

Books in Print with Book Reviews Plus/Europe. *Producer:* R.R. Bowker Electronic Publishing. *Operating System:* PC. *Subject:* Reading/Book Reviews. *Price:* See distributor. *Grade Level:* JH, HS, C. *Hardware:* IBM PC or compatible; 512K RAM (640K recommended); CD-ROM player; two floppy disk drives (hard disk recommended); and printer. *Software:* PC-DOS or MS-DOS 3.0 or higher; Microsoft CD-ROM extensions. *Distributor:* EBSCO.

Citations to over 500,000 books declared to be out of print or out of stock (July

1979 to date) from roughly 22,000 publishers. Subject classification scheme uses over 65,000 Library of Congress subject headings. Corresponds to *Books Out of Print* and partly to *Books in Print* online database.

Bookshelf/Microsoft. *Producer:* Microsoft Corporation. *Operating System:* PC. *Subject:* Reference. *Price:* $295. *Grade Level:* JH, HS, C. *Hardware:* IBM PC, XT, AT, or compatible; 640K RAM; CD-ROM player; monitor; printer (optional). *Software:* PC-DOS or MS-DOS 3.1 or higher, Microsoft CD-ROM extensions. *Distributor:* EBSCO.

The CD-ROM reference library and word processing tool includes complete versions of the *American Heritage Dictionary, Rogets II Electronic Thesaurus, The 1987 World Almanac and Book of Facts, Bartlett's Familiar Quotations, The Chicago Manual of Style, Houghton Mifflin Usage Alert, U.S. Zip Code Directory, Forms and Letters, Business Information Sources, Houghton Mifflin Speller.* Bookshelf works within the word processor as you are writing and is fully compatible with many popular word processor programs.

Britannica Family Choice. *Producer:* Britannica. *Operating System:* PC. *Subject:* General reference. *Price:* $199. *Grade Level:* Elem., JH, HS. *Hardware:* See distributor. *Software:* See distributor. *Distributor:* Updata.

Contains 15 educational software programs for children: Algebra I First Semester and Algebra II Second Semester, the Berenstain Bears Junior Jigsaw (10 puzzles), the Berenstain Bears Learn About Counting (basic math concepts), Body Transparent (movable bones of human body), Designasaurus (award winner for Best Educational Program 1988), Grammar Examiner (gain grammar skills while editing a newspaper), Jigsaw! The Ultimate Electronic Puzzle (for the whole family), Just Fax (creates fax cover sheets for business or home office use), Math Maze, Millionaire II (gain stock market insight), Revolution '76 (economic and military strategy), States and Traits (lakes, mountains, etc.), Super Spellicopter (spelling game), Fiction Advisor (provides list of recommended books and authors based on areas of study or interest).

Bug Adventure: An Insect Adventure. *Operating System:* DOS. *Subject:* Entomology. *Grade Level:* K–2. *Hardware:* See distributor. *Software:* See distributor. *Distributor:* Updata.

Journey into the insect kingdom. Contains photographs and full-motion video. Covers life span, range, social habits, diet, senses and other insect attributes.

Career Opportunities. Quanta Press, Inc., 1313 Fifth Street, Suite SE 223A, Minneapolis, MN 55414; 612/379-3956. *Fax:* 612/623-4570. *Price:* $69.95. *Platform:* Macintosh, DOS. *Grade Level:* HS. *Curriculum:* Reference and Interdisciplinary.

Helps individuals make career choices. Included are job titles, job descriptions, education levels, advancement chances, average salaries and working conditions.

The Causes of World War I. *Operating System:* DOS, MAC, Windows. *Subject:* WWI. *Grade Level:* General. *Hardware:* See distributor. *Software:* See distributor. *Distributor:* Updata.

Explores the political, economic, and social factors and events that gave rise to the war. Contains an audio-visual presentation with text linked to a 24-volume student encyclopedia and glossary.

The Causes of World War II. Operating System: DOS, MAC, Windows. *Subject:* WWII. *Grade Level:* General. *Hardware:* See distributor. *Software:* See distributor. *Distributor:* Updata.

Explore how the events and consequences of WWI sowed the seeds for a new conflict. Chronicles the rise to power of new totalitarian regimes and the events that led to global conflict.

CD Audio Stack. Producer: Voyager. *Operating System:* MAC. *Subject:* Music. *Price:* $99.95. *Grade Level:* JH, HS. *Hardware:* See distributor. *Software:* See distributor. *Distributor:* CDiscovery.

Audio CD's are controlled from Hypercard with this utility that allows you to play music, sounds, or spoken words including Audio Event Maker, Audio Ideas, and an on-line manual.

CD Calculus. John Wiley and Sons, Inc., 605 Third Avenue, New York, NY 10158; 212/850-6172. *Fax:* 212/850-6799. *Price:* $49.95. *Platform:* DOS. *Grade Level:* HS. *Curriculum:* Mathematics.

Consists of the entire text of *Calculus with Analytic Geometry,* 4th Ed. by Howard Anton.

CD Coreworks. Roth Publishing Inc., 185 Great Neck Road, Great Neck, NY 11021; 800/899-7684. *Fax:* 516/829-7746. *Tech. Support:* 800/899-7684. *Price:* $475. *Platform:* DOS. *Grade Level:* HS. *Curriculum:* Language Arts.

Integrates four poetry indexes in a single disk, providing a definitive index to more than 140,000 poems and over 25,000 essays, 4,000 short stories and 850 plays in the English language.

CD 7. Producer: Quantum Leap Technology. *Operating System:* MAC. *Subject:* Entertainment. *Price:* $99. *Grade Level:* JH, HS. *Hardware:* Any Macintosh. *Software:* See distributor. *Distributor:* EBSCO.

Large collection of Macintosh software including over 14,000 files — 2,570 art, 931 games, 838 Hypercard stacks, 1,262 demo files, 1,180 digitized sounds, 1,453 music files, over 1,000 Macintosh utilities and more.

CD-Gene. Producer: Software Toolworks. *Operating System:* PC. *Subject:* Science. *Price:* $949. *Grade Level:* HS. *Hardware:* See distributor. *Software:* See distributor. *Distributor:* Bureau of Electronic Publishing.

A genetic sequencing database that contains current versions of four leading DNA and amino acid sequence databases such as GenBank, EMBL and Swiss Prot and Protein Identification Resource.

CD Sourcebook of American History. Operating System: DOS, MAC, Windows. *Subject:* American History. *Grade Level:* General. *Hardware:* See distributor. *Software:* See distributor. *Distributor:* Updata.

A comprehensive reference library of history containing over 600 source documents.

Cell Ebration. Operating System: MAC. *Subject:* Science. *Price:* $289. *Grade Level:* Elem. *Hardware:* See distributor. *Software:* See distributor. *Distributor:* CD-ROM, Inc.

The first program in a new multimedia-based science curriculum.

"Cell"ebration. Science for Kids Inc., 9950 Concord Church Road, Lewisville, NC 27023; 910/945-9000. *Fax:* 910/945-2500. *Tech. Support:* 910/945-9000. *Price:* $289. *Platform:* Macintosh. *Grade Level:* Primary, Elementary. *Curriculum:* Science.

An interactive multimedia science learning system that includes lesson guides, teacher's manual, hands-on activities, microscope, magnifying glass and 15 slides.

"Cell"Ebration. *Operating System:* MAC, MPC. *Subject:* Cell Biology. *Grade Level:* K–2. *Hardware:* See distributor. *Software:* See distributor. *Distributor:* Updata.

Explore the cell and learn the characteristics and processes of living organisms. Investigate organisms with prepared slides, a magnifying glass and microscopes. Features full color photographs, natural sounds and voices, graphics, music, etc.

Census Data. *Operating System:* PC. *Subject:* Census. *Price:* $995. *Grade Level:* JH, HS. *Hardware:* See distributor. *Software:* See distributor. *Distributor:* Bureau of Electronic Publishing.

Contains 100+ key variables from the 1990 census by census tract, zip code, place, county, and state for the United States. Data includes key areas such as population by race, sex, age, origin.

Chemistry. *Producer:* Queue. *Operating System:* PC. *Subject:* Chemistry. *Price:* $175. *Grade Level:* HS, C. *Hardware:* See distributor. *Software:* See distributor. *Distributor:* CDiscovery.

Four highly rated chemistry programs from COMPress, Program Design International, Intellectual Software, and Silwa. The titles include: Concepts in General Chemistry — chemical reactions, chemical stoichiometry, ionic equilibrium, mole concept, oxidation-reduction reactions, reaction in aqueous solution; Chemistry Package — elementary chemistry, chemical symbols, general chemistry I & II, chemistry challenge, chemical vocabulary building I, basic inorganic terminology, inorganic nomenclature II and review questions in chemistry; Acid-Base Chemistry — atomic structure, chemical formulas and equation, solutions, physical chemistry, and organic chemistry.

Children's Favorite Stories, Poems, and Fairy Tales. *Producer:* Queue. *Operating System:* MAC. *Subject:* Literature. *Price:* $95. *Grade Level:* K–4. *Hardware:* See distributor. *Software:* See distributor. *Distributor:* CDiscovery.

Children in grades K–4 will be challenged and entertained by a collection of readings that feature popular stories by famous authors. They include five of the most popular Beatrix Potter animal tales; the classics *Little Red Riding Hood, Cinderella, Jack and the Beanstalk,* and *The Velveteen Rabbit;* two volumes of popular Mother Goose nursery rhymes, and a collection of children's poems and songs.

Children's Treasury of Stories, Nursery Rhymes, and Songs. *Operating System:* DOS, MAC. *Subject:* Children's Literature. *Grade Level:* Preschool to grade 2. *Hardware:* See distributor. *Software:* See distributor. *Distributor:* Updata.

An interactive multimedia collection designed to educate beginning readers. Contains nursery rhymes, including "Hush-a-Bye Baby," "Mary Had a Little Lamb," "Jack and Jill," "Little Bo-Peep," and "Three Little Kittens" as well as eight classic children's songs: "Farmer in the Dell," "Old MacDonald," etc.

CIA World Fact Book. Quanta Press Inc., 1313 Fifth Street, Suite SE 223A, Minneapolis, MN 55414; 612/623-4570. *Price:* $49.95. *Platform:* Macintosh, DOS. *Grade Level:* JH, HS. *Curriculum:* Social Studies.

A reference disk of the U.S. government's own almanac containing 249 countries, territories and islands around the world.

The CIA World Factbook. *Operating System:* DOS, MAC. *Subject:* Geography, People, Government, Economics, Communications, Defense Forces. *Grade Level:* General. *Hardware:* See distributor. *Software:* See distributor. *Distributor:* Updata.

Uses the Federal government's own world almanac, providing profiles on 249 countries, territories and islands around the world. The sub-directory contains the 249 maps, representing each profiled country, territory and island.

Cinderella. *Operating System:* MAC. *Subject:* Literature/Stories. *Price:* $69. *Grade Level:* Elem. *Hardware:* See distributor. *Software:* See distributor. *Distributor:* CD-ROM, Inc.

Cinderella still marries the prince, but she also finds rooms in the palace for her two stepsisters.

Classic Library. *Operating System:* MAC, Windows. *Subject:* Literature. *Grade Level:* JH to Adult. *Hardware:* See distributor. *Software:* See distributor. *Distributor:* Updata.

Includes works and biographies of 247 authors, from Aesop and William Blake to Oscar Wilde and William Yeats.

Coate's Art Review: Impressionism. Quanta Press, Inc., 1313 Fifth Street, Suite SE 223A, Minneapolis, MN 55414; 612/379-3956. *Fax:* 612/623-4570. *Price:* $79.95. *Platform:* Macintosh, DOS. *Grade Level:* HS. *Curriculum:* Arts and Music.

A comprehensive look at all major artists and artworks of the Impressionist era. Includes background information as well as museum and collection data.

College Boards Queue. *Producer:* College Board. *Operating System:* MAC. *Subject:* Study Skills. *Price:* $195. *Grade Level:* HS, C. *Hardware:* See distributor. *Software:* See distributor. *Distributor:* CDiscovery.

Complete package to prepare students for the English SAT and ACT tests, plus the English, history, and biology achievement tests.

The College Handbook. Macmillian New Media, 124 Mount Auburn Street, Cambridge, MA 02138; 800/342-1338; 617/661-2955. *Fax:* 617/661-2403. *Tech. Support:* 800/342-1338. *Price:* $39.95. *Platform:* DOS. *Grade Level:* HS. *Curriculum:* Reference and Interdisciplinary.

Contains information on more than 2,700 colleges to help students pinpoint the right college.

The Columbia Granger's World of Poetry. *Operating Systems:* DOS, MAC, Windows. *Subject:* Poetry. *Grade Level:* General. *Hardware:* See distributor. *Software:* See distributor. *Distributor:* Updata.

Locate more than 135,000 poems by more than 20,000 poets, in more than 700 anthologies and 72 volumes of collected and selected works. Detailed descriptions and evaluations of every anthology included.

The Comic Creator. *Operating Systems:* MAC, MPC. *Subjects:* Art, design. *Grade Level:* General. *Hardware:* See distributor. *Software:* See distributor. *Distributor:* Updata.
Write, design, print and store your original comic books.

Complete Guide to Special Interest Videos. Quanta Press Inc., 1313 Fifth Street, Suite SE 223A, Minneapolis, MN 55414; 612/379-3956. *Fax:* 612/623-4570. *Price:* $49.95. *Platform:* Macintosh, DOS. *Grade Level:* HS. *Curriculum:* Social Studies.
A listing of over 9,000 videos, organized by title and by subject. An order form is included for any of the videos.

Complete House. Deep River Publishing, P.O. Box 9715-975, Portland, ME 04104; 800/643-5630; 207/871-1684. *Fax:* 207/871-1683. *Tech. Support:* 207/871-1684. *Price:* $39.95. *Platform:* Macintosh, MPC. *Grade Level:* HS. *Curriculum:* Arts and Music.
Features House Design — an in-depth look at the relationship of home-owner, environment and house. Also, Kitchen and Bath Design — gets right down to plan and construction of the kitchen. CAD/FP as a drawing package includes 20 complete floor plans.

Complete Multimedia Bible. *Operating System:* Windows. *Subject:* Religion. *Grade Level:* General. *Hardware:* See distributor. *Software:* See distributor. *Distributor:* Updata.
The complete Bible (King James version) with biblical maps, inspirational video, and narration. All of the bible is cross referenced by topic, idea, definition or history.

Composer Quest. *Operating System:* MPC. *Subject:* Music/History. *Price:* $74.95. *Grade Level:* General. *Hardware:* See distributor. *Software:* See distributor. *Distributor:* New Media Source.
Interactive multimedia package which contains CD-quality recordings of great musical performances. History of music from 17th through 20th centuries. Games provide additional entertainment.

Composer Quest. *Operating System:* MPC. *Subjects:* Music, History. *Grade Level:* General. *Hardware:* See distributor. *Software:* See distributor. *Distributor:* Updata.
Discover great composers in classical and early jazz music in this interactive multimedia tour of music history. Features biographies, new events, a music trivia game, quizzes, coverage of important eras in history, etc.

Comprehensive Review in Biology. *Producer:* Queue. *Operating Systems:* MAC/PC. *Subject:* Study Skills/Guidance. *Price:* $295. *Grade Level:* HS, C. *Hardware:* See distributor. *Software:* See distributor. *Distributor:* CDiscovery.
A compilation of programs that offer extensive reviews and practice in biology. The titles include: Comprehensive Review in Biology Package, Biology I and II, Advanced Placement Biology Test Preparation, CBAT Biology, and SEI Biology.

Compton's Interactive Encyclopedia. Compton's NewMedia, Inc., 2320 Camino Vida Roble, Carlsbad, CA 92009; 800/862-2206; 800/216-6116 (catalog sales); 619/929-2500. *Fax:* 619/929-2555. *Tech Support:* 619/929-2626. *Price:* $149.95. *Platform:* Macintosh, Windows. *Grade Level:* Elementary, JH. *Curriculum:* Reference and Interdisciplinary.

All 26 volumes of *Compton's Encyclopedia* including 9 million words in 32,000 articles, 13,000 images, maps and graphs, 5,000 charts and diagrams, 43 animated sequences and 60 minutes of music, speech and other sound.

Compton's Interactive Encyclopedia. *Operating Systems:* MAC, MPC. *Subject:* General Reference. *Grade Level:* General. *Hardware:* See distributor. *Software:* See distributor. *Distributor:* Updata.

A new interactive multimedia encyclopedia. Has a "Virtual Workspace" feature which expands your computer's desktop capabilities as if the screen extended beyond its physical boundaries. Features the full text and graphics of *Compton's Encyclopedia* and *Merriam Webster Online Dictionary and Thesaurus.*

Compton's Multi-Media Encyclopedia. *Operating Systems:* DOS, MAC, MPC. *Subject:* General Reference. *Grade Level:* General. *Hardware:* See distributor. *Software:* See distributor. *Distributor:* Updata.

This multimedia encyclopedia with mouse-driven commands contains the full texts of 33,700 articles. The audio capability allows students to hear famous speeches which are actually spoken and defined for users.

The Constitution Papers. *Operating System:* DOS. *Subject:* American Historical Documents. *Grade Level:* General. *Hardware:* See distributor. *Software:* See distributor. *Distributor:* Updata.

Contains the most historic American documents (The Constitution, Washington's Farewell Address), and many of the documents that helped to shape our constitution originally (Virginia [Randolph] Plan; the Federalist Papers; New Jersey [Paterson] Plan; Hamilton's Plan of Union). There are many documents that helped shape the United States, from the writings that incited the American colonists to sever with England.

County-City Plus. *Operating System:* PC. *Subject:* Reference. *Price:* $195. *Grade Level:* General. *Hardware:* See distributor. *Software:* See distributor. *Distributor:* EBSCO.

An annual update and extension of the data in the Census Bureau's popular *County and City Databook* containing county summaries (data for every county and state), city statistics and data for places.

Consumer Information. Quanta Press, Inc., 1313 Fifth Street, Suite SE 223A, Minneapolis, MN 55414, 612/379-3956. *Fax:* 612/623-4570. *Price:* $49.95. *Platform:* Macintosh, DOS. *Grade Level:* HS. *Curriculum:* Reference and Interdisciplinary.

Lists most of the books and publications currently available from the Federal Government Consumer Information Center at Pueblo, Colorado. It covers subjects ranging from children to travel, and anything in between.

Contemporary Authors. Gale Research, Inc., 835 Penobscot Building, Detroit, MI 48226-4094; 800/877-GALE; 313/961-2242. *Fax:* 313/961-6083. *Tech. Support:* 800/877-4253, Ext. 6021. *Price:* Single User — $3,500; Updates 2×/year — $650; Lease/year — $795. *Platform:* DOS. *Grade Level:* HS. *Curriculum:* Language Arts.

An authoritative source of biographical and bibliographical information on important authors of our time. Includes the full text of *Contemporary Authors*, Vol. 1–40, *Contemporary Authors New Revision Series*, Vol. 1–41 and *Contemporary Authors Permanent Series*, Vol. 1–2.

Countries of the World. Bureau for Electronic Publishing, 141 New Road, Parsippany, NJ 07054; 800/828-4766 (orders); 201/808-2700. *Fax:* 201/808-2676. *Tech. Support:* 201/808-2700, Ext. 22. *Price:* $495; $69 single CD-ROM. *Platform:* Macintosh, DOS. *Grade Level:* HS. *Curriculum:* Social Studies.

Detailed information on population, society, environment, foreign relations, geography, religion, agriculture, economy, etc., taken from 106 different *U.S. Army Country Handbooks.*

Countries of the World Encyclopedia. *Operating Systems:* DOS, MAC. *Subject:* International Statistics. *Grade Level:* JH to Adult. *Hardware:* See distributor. *Software:* See distributor. *Distributor:* Updata.

Contains a variety of data about different nations. Also presents up-to-date information provided by the 151 U.S. embassies around the world.

Creepy Crawlies. Media Design Interactive, The Old Hop Kiln, 1 Long Garden Walk, Farnham, Surrey, GU9 7HP England; 011-44-252-737630. *Fax:* 011-44-252-710948. *Tech. Support:* 800/654-8802. *Price:* $69. *Platform:* Macintosh, MPC. *Grade Level:* JH, HS. *Curriculum:* Science.

The world of bugs designed for kids. Also defines and classifies lower animals according to biological taxonomy.

Criterion Goes to the Movies. *Operating Systems:* MAC, Windows. *Subject:* Film. *Grade Level:* General. *Hardware:* See distributor. *Software:* See distributor. *Distributor:* Updata.

A detailed buyer's guide for videos. Contains synopses, detailed essays, special features information, credits, and QuickTime movie clips of over 150 classic films sold in videodisc editions.

Current Biography on CD-ROM. *Subject:* Reference/General Biography. *Price:* $189. *Grade Level:* General. *Distributor:* H.W. Wilson.

Searchable biographies for 12 years of newsmakers and more. More than 2,000 full text biographies and 1,800 obituaries. Instant access by name, profession, gender and more.

Darwin. *Operating Systems:* MAC/PC. *Subject:* Reference, Science. *Price:* $89. *Grade Level:* JH, HS. *Hardware:* See distributor. *Software:* See distributor. *Distributor:* CD-ROM, Inc.

The collected works of Charles Darwin. A guide to teaching about Darwin for all ages.

Dinosaur Safari. Creative Multimedia, 514 NW 11th Avenue, Suite 203, Portland, OR 97209; 800/262-7668; 503/241-4351. *Fax:* 503/241-4370. *Tech. Support:* 503/241-1530. *Price:* $69.99. *Platform:* MPC, Macintosh. *Grade Level:* Elem., JH, HS. *Curriculum:* Science.

Travel back in time to the Mesozoic Era with this dinosaur adventure game while learning about dinosaurs, geography, flora, fauna and geology. Included are 310 locations in five time periods, 100 species of Mesozoic plants and 60 live action, animated creatures.

Discis. *Producer:* Discus. *Operating System:* MAC. *Subject:* Reading. *Price:* $750. *Grade Level:* K, Elem. *Hardware:* See distributor. *Software:* See distributor. *Distributor:* CDiscovery.

Appropriate for kindergarten to grade 6 reading level, the Discis 10-book library includes books by well-known children's authors, such as: Beatrix Potter, *The Tale of Peter Rabbit* ($85), *The Tale of Benjamin Bunny* ($70); Robert Munsch, *Thomas Snowsuit* ($75), *Mud Puddle* ($75), *The Paper Bag Princess* ($70); *Cinderella*, the original fairy tale ($70); *Scary Poems for Rotten Kids* ($85) by Sean O'Hugin; *A Long Hard Day on the Ranch* ($70) by Audrey Nelson; *Heather Hits Her First Home Run* ($85) by Ted Plantos; and *Moving Gives Me a Stomach Ache* ($85) by Heather McKend. Discis books appear on a screen as actual pages of a book with text and illustrations enhanced with voices, music and sound effects. (Discis books can be purchased separately.)

Don Quixote. Ebook Inc., 32970 Alvarado-Niles Road, Suite 704, Union City, CA 94587; 510/429-1331. *Fax:* 510/429-1394. *Tech. Support:* 510/713-8904. *Price:* $29.95. *Platform:* MPC. *Grade Level:* JH, HS. *Curriculum:* Language Arts.

Don Quixote and his faithful companion, Sancho Panza, set out to rid the world of the Devil. This classic tale of humanity comes to life with vivid illustrations, music and lively narration.

Down to Earth. *Operating System:* MAC. *Subject:* Science. *Price:* $249. *Grade Level:* General. *Hardware:* Macintosh Plus/SEII/portable 1MB RAM. *Software:* 6.0.0. *Distributor:* Updata.

A collection of environmental pictures of foliage, landscape, marine environments, and more.

Econ/Stats I. *Producer:* Hopkins Technology. *Operating System:* PC. *Subject:* Reference/Economics. *Price:* $65. *Grade Level:* HS, C. *Hardware:* IBM PC or compatible; 512K RAM; CD-ROM player. *Software:* PC-DOS or MS-DOS version 3.1, 3.3 or higher, Microsoft CD-ROM extensions. *Distributor:* EBSCO.

Contains Consumer Price Index (320 commodities and services, 50 area definitions), Producer Price Index (over 6,700 commodities), Export-Import Price Index (over 3,000 products and services), Industrial Production Index (272 commodities), Money Stock, Selected Interest Rates (90 Rates), Industry Employment hours and Earnings by State and Areas (527 industries, 374 area definitions nearly a half-million records), and capacity Utilization (38 industrial categories). Some data goes back to 1913.

Education Library. *Producer:* SilverPlatter. *Operating System:* PC/MAC. *Subject:* Reference. *Price:* $450 annual. *Grade Level:* General. *Hardware:* See distributor. *Software:* See distributor. *Distributor:* Updata.

An international bibliography of educational materials, containing approximately 500,000 records on all types of materials, including books, journals, theses, data files, slides, newspapers, recordings, filmstrips, microforms, and manuscripts.

Electricity and Magnetism. Cambrix Publishing, 6269 Variel Avenue, Suite B, Woodland Hills, CA 91367; 818/992-8484. *Fax:* 818/992-8781. *Tech. Support:* 818/992-8484. *Price:* $49.95. *Platform:* DOS. *Grade Level:* HS. *Curriculum:* Science.

An interactive disk with hundreds of animations, photographs and diagrams of the world of electricity and magnetism. Users can activate animations which show how electrical current flows around a circuit or how a lightning conductor works.

Electronic Encyclopedia of WWII. Marshall Cavendish Corp., 2415 Jerusalem Avenue, P.O. Box 587, North Bellmore, NY 11710; 800/821-9881. *Fax:* 516/785-8133. *Tech. Support:* 800/643-4351. *Price:* $379.95, single users; $895, network 50 users. *Platform:* DOS. *Grade Level:* HS. *Curriculum:* Social Studies.

A chronological and comprehensive history of the Second World War. Includes the full text of the print *Encyclopedia of World War II.*

European Monarchs. Quanta Press, Inc., 1313 Fifth Street, Suite SE 223A, Minneapolis, MN 55414; 612/379-3956. *Fax:* 612/623-4570. *Price:* $79.95. *Platform:* Macintosh, DOS. *Grade Level:* HS. *Curriculum:* Social Studies.

Historical database of information related to the monarchs of Europe. Contains records of kings and queens from over 20 European nations (past and present). Also includes 16 black and white sketches of selected monarchs.

Everywhere USA Travel Guide. Deep River Publishing, P.O. Box 9715-975, Portland, ME 04104; 800/643-5630; 207/871-1684. *Fax:* 207/871-1683. *Tech. Support:* 207/871-1684. *Price:* $59.95. *Platform:* Macintosh, MPC. *Grade Level:* JH, HS. *Curriculum:* Reference and Interdisciplinary.

Thousands of U.S. tourist sites with an easy interface for viewing attractions.

The Family Doctor. Creative Multimedia, 514 NW 11th Avenue, Suite 203, Portland, OR 97209; 800/262-7668; 503/241-4351. *Fax:* 503/241-4370. *Tech. Support:* 503/241-1530. *Price:* $79.99. *Platform:* Macintosh, MPC. *Grade Level:* JH, HS. *Curriculum:* Health.

Over 240 color images illustrating human anatomy, diseases, common medical procedures and brand name drugs. The full-text "Family Doctor" column covers 1,500 common questions. Also included is a consumer guide to 1,600 prescription drugs showing uses and side effects.

Favorite Folk Tales. *Producer:* Queue. *Operating System:* MAC. *Subject:* Literature. *Price:* $95. *Grade Level:* Elem., JH, HS. *Hardware:* See distributor. *Software:* See distributor. *Distributor:* CDiscovery.

A collection of folk tales from around the globe including stories from North America — Eskimo, Hopi, and African American tales, Europe, the Far East, and Mexico, plus Paul Bunyan stories, and Paul Kipling's *Just So Stories* with sound and music.

Federal Grants/Funding Locator. Staff Directories, Ltd., P.O. Box 62, Mount Vernon, VA 22121-0062; 703/739-0900. *Fax:* 703/739-0234. *Tech. Support:* 703/739-0900, Ext. 218. *Price:* $295. *Platform:* DOS, Windows. *Grade Level:* HS. *Curriculum:* General.

Provides detailed information on every grant or funding program by a federal agency, over 1,400 programs covering topics from AIDS to Zoology with funds for individual schools, non-profit, etc.

Food/Analyst Plus. Hopkins Technology, 421 Hazel Lane, Hopkins, MN 55343-7116; 800/397-9211. *Fax:* 612/931-9377. *Tech. Support:* 800/397-9211. *Price:* $199. *Platform:* DOS. *Grade Level:* HS. *Curriculum:* Health.

A complete nutritional analysis program which reports food calories, fat, sugar, protein, cholesterol, vitamins and more. Contains 23,000 foods with 100 nutrients.

include migration, contact with settlers, wars, social structure, treaties, means of sustenance, agriculture, tools, clothing, arts and crafts, religious and spiritual beliefs as well as legends and rituals.

American Journey 1896–1945. Operating System: DOS. *Subject:* American History. *Grade Level:* JH to Adult. *Hardware:* See distributor. *Software:* See distributor. *Distributor:* Updata.

Study America's emergence as a world power between 1896 and 1945. Uses nearly 1,000 photographs, over an hour of audio and a high-tech timeline to bring the Gay Nineties, the Roaring Twenties, the Depression, and the war years to life.

American Visions: 20th Century Art. Operating System: MAC, Windows. *Subject:* American Art. *Grade Level:* JH to Adult. *Hardware:* See distributor. *Software:* See distributor. *Distributor:* Updata.

Presents 189 works from 129 American artists in 24-bit color along with videos, photographs and narratives about their work.

The American West: Myth and Reality. Operating System: DOS, MAC, and Windows. *Subject:* History. *Grade Level:* General. *Hardware:* See distributor. *Software:* See distributor. *Distributor:* Updata.

Presents an interactive history of the American West. Demonstrates how more than 100 years of fantasy about the West has made it difficult to distinguish historical fact from myth. Contains an audio-visual presentation with text linked to a 24-volume student encyclopedia and glossary.

Americans in Space. Operating System: Mac, MPC. *Subject:* Space Exploration. *Grade Level:* General. *Hardware:* See distributor. *Software:* See distributor. *Distributor:* Updata.

Contains the entire history of American space exploration. Presents almost 600 pictures and more than an hour of video.

Anatomist. Operating System: MAC. *Subject:* Science. *Price:* $295. *Grade Level:* General. *Hardware:* See distributor. *Software:* See distributor. *Distributor:* CD-ROM, Inc.

Based on *The Anatomy Coloring Book* by Harper & Row, this package allows you to move through the body as you learn names, details, and see color images.

Ancient Greece. Operating System: DOS, MAC. *Subject:* History. *Grade Level:* JH to Adult. *Hardware:* See distributor. *Software:* See distributor. *Distributor:* Updata.

Learn about the mythology, art, architecture, government, philosophy, literature, social order and routines of daily life in ancient Greece. Contains hundreds of photos and original drawings, as well as general category search, index and a timeline index.

Animal Alphabet. Operating System: MPC, MAC. *Subject:* Education, reading skills. *Grade Level:* K–1. *Hardware:* See distributor. *Software:* See distributor. *Distributor:* Updata.

Designed to help children learn to read. Full of hidden surprises and musical interludes.

Freshe Arte. Quanta Press, Inc., 1313 Fifth Street, Suite SE 223A, Minneapolis, MN 55414; 612/379-3956. *Fax:* 612/623-4570. *Price:* $99.95. *Platform:* Macintosh, DOS. *Grade Level:* HS. *Curriculum:* Arts and Music.

Public domain clip art — over 1,500 images in 600dpi, royalty free; includes a section of art created by children.

Gale Research Inc.: Gale's Discovering Authors CD-ROM. *Producer:* Gale. *Operating System:* PC/MAC. *Subject:* Reference/Literature. *Price:* $500. *Grade Level:* HS, C. *Hardware:* Compatible with all major CD-ROM. *Software:* None. *Distributor:* Gale Research, Inc.

Full-text biographical essays on 300 authors, critical essays on their writings, a bibliography of their works, a list of other sources of information on the author; and a summary of media adaptations of their works. In other words, everything you need to know about an author. An update is planned every three years.

Gale's Literary Index. Gale Research, Inc., 835 Penobscot Building, Detroit, MI 48226-4094; 800/877-GALE; 313/961-2242. *Fax:* 313/961-6083. *Tech. Support:* 800/877-4253, Ext. 6021. *Price:* $149. *Platform:* DOS. *Grade Level:* HS. *Curriculum:* Language Arts.

Combines various indexes from 32 literary series including *Contemporary Authors, Nineteenth Century Literary Criticism* and *Contemporary Literary Criticism.* The disk indexes biographies and criticisms of over 110,000 authors and 120,000 titles.

Games in Japanese. (Playing with Language Series) Syracuse Language Systems, 719 East Genesee Street, Syracuse, NY 13210; 315/478-6729. *Fax:* 315/478-6902. *Tech. Support:* 800/688-1937. *Price:* $39.95. *Platform:* MPC. *Grade Level:* Elem., JH. *Curriculum:* Foreign Language.

Multimedia games offering students an exciting way to practice, learn and use language.

A German Requiem. *Producer:* Warner New Media. *Operating System:* MAC. *Subject:* Music/Brahms. *Price:* $70.50. *Grade Level:* JH, HS, C. *Hardware:* IBM RAM, hard disk drive/5–7MB free MAC compatible CD-ROM drive. *Software:* MAC system software 6.0.5 or higher. *Distributor:* EBSCO.

Greatest choral work of the Romantic era, Johannes Brahms' "A German Requiem" is performed brilliantly in this two-disk set, with Robert Shaw conducting the Atlanta Symphony Orchestra and with Robert Shaw conducting the Atlanta Symphony Orchestra and Chorus. Pictures, commentaries, additional music, analysis, historical information, musical glossary, and index are all interactively accessible with a Macintosh computer. Use the Requiem Map to get instant access to any part of the music — including all the themes and their transformations; take more than 50 side journeys to enhance your musical experience with richly illustrated biographical, historical, and musical highlights; enhance your understanding of music with more than 500 examples of sound and music from Gregorian Chant to Britten's War Requiem; try the Harmonic Plan and explore how Brahms used harmony.

Ghost Tracks. *Operating System:* PC. *Subject:* Literature. *Price:* $65. *Grade Level:* JH, HS. *Hardware:* See distributor. *Software:* See distributor. *Distributor:* CD-ROM, Inc.

Five hundred and one classic tales of horror, mystery and the fantastic. One hundred thirty authors including Dickens, Bierce, Poe, Stoker and Twain. Accompanying illustrations and an oversized print mode for the visually impaired.

Great Cities of the World Vol. 1. InterOptica Publishing Ltd., 300 Montgomery Street, Suite 201, San Francisco, CA 94104; 800/708-7827 (orders); 415/788-8788. *Fax:* 415/788-8886. *Tech. Support:* 212/941-2988. *Price:* $49.95. *Platform:* Macintosh, Windows. *Grade Level:* JH, HS. *Curriculum:* Social Studies.

Covers Bombay, Cairo, London, Los Angeles, Moscow, New York, Paris, Rio de Janeiro, Sydney and Tokyo plus climate, currency, local times, phrases, culture, sights, transport, shopping, entertainment, recreation, restaurants, hotels and travel planner.

Great Cities of the World Vol. 2. InterOptica Publishing Ltd., 300 Montgomery Street, Suite 201, San Francisco, CA 94104; 800/708-7827 (orders); 415/788-8788. *Fax:* 415/788-8886. *Tech. Support:* 212/941-2988. *Price:* $49.95. *Platform:* Macintosh, Windows. *Grade Level:* JH, HS. *Curriculum:* Social Studies.

Covers Berlin, Buenos Aires, Chicago, Jerusalem, Johannesburg, Rome, San Francisco, Seoul, Singapore and Toronto.

Great Literature Plus. Bureau for Electronic Publishing, 141 New Road, Parsippany, NJ 07054; 800/828-4766 (orders); 201/808-2700. *Fax:* 201/808-2767. *Tech. Support:* 201/808-2700, ext. 22. *Price:* $99. *Platform:* Macintosh, DOS, MPC. *Grade Level:* HS. *Curriculum:* Language Arts.

The full text of 943 classic works of literature. It includes 31 biographies, journals, letters, 21 literary criticisms, 32 historical documents, 75 essays, 461 poems, 199 fictional works, 10 religious documents and 27 science and education books.

Great Wonders of the World Vol. 1. InterOptica Publishing Ltd., 300 Montgomery Street, Suite 201, San Francisco, CO 94104; 800/708-7827 (orders); 415/788-8788. *Fax:* 415/788-8886. *Tech. Support:* 212/941-2988. *Price:* $99.95. *Platform:* Macintosh, Windows. *Grade Level:* JH, HS. *Curriculum:* Social Studies.

Man-made wonders of the world such as the Empire State Building, Angkor Wat, Great Wall of China, Inca Ruins, Panama Canal, Pyramids, Taj Mahal, trans–Siberian Railway, and Venice.

Great Wonders of the World Vol. 2 Natural Wonders. InterOptica Publishing Ltd., 300 Montgomery Street, Suite 201, San Francisco, CA 94104; 800/708-7827 (orders); 415/788-8788. *Fax:* 415/788-8886. *Tech. Support:* 212/941-2988. *Price:* $99.95. *Platform:* Macintosh, Windows. *Grade Level:* JH, HS. *Curriculum:* Social Studies.

Over 350 illustrations, maps and photographs. Includes 500 pages of text for Natural Wonders of the World such as the Great Barrier Reef, Indian Monsoon, Mount Everest, Grand Canyon, Amazon Rain Forest, Wild Beast Migration, and the Blue Whale.

Grolier Multimedia Electronic Encyclopedia. 1736 Westwood Boulevard, Los Angeles, CA 90024; 800/882-2844. *Price:* Varies. *Grade Level:* Elem. to HS. *Curriculum:* Reference. *Distributor:* Updata.

Full text word search. Video/Audio clips.

Heart: The Engine of Life. Updata Publications, Inc., 1736 Westwood Boulevard,

Los Angeles, CA 90024; 800/882-2844. *Fax:* 310/474-4095. *Tech. Support:* 800/882-2844. *Price:* $99. *Platform:* DOS. *Grade Level:* JH, HS. *Curriculum:* Health.

An animated color tutorial that interacts with the user. Everything you ever wanted to know about the heart and how it functions.

Heather Hits Her First Home Run. *Operating System:* MAC. *Subject:* Literature/ Stories. *Price:* $84. *Grade Level:* Elem. *Hardware:* See distributor. *Software:* See distributor. *Distributor:* CD-ROM, Inc.

The pressure is on Heather to save the game and she goes through many different emotions as she stands at the plate.

History of the World. Bureau for Electronic Publishing, 141 New Road, Parsippany, NJ 07054; 800/828-4766 (orders); 201/808-2676. *Tech. Support:* 201/808-2700, Ext. 22. *Price:* $79.95. *Platform:* Macintosh, DOS. *Grade Level:* HS. *Curriculum:* Social Studies.

Based on two best-selling textbooks from HarperCollins, this title spans the history of the world from Caesar to the Apollo space missions.

Illustrated Facts: How the World Works. XIPHIAS, 8758 Venice Boulevard, Los Angeles, CA 90034; 800/421-9194 (sales); 310/841-2790. *Fax:* 310/841-2559. *Price:* $39.95. *Platform:* Macintosh, MPC. *Grade Level:* HS. *Curriculum:* Social Studies.

A compilation of 70 video clips that takes an entertaining look at man's endeavors in the areas of justice, warfare, money, media, lifestyle, enterprise and government.

Illustrated Facts: How Things Work. XIPHIAS, 8758 Venice Boulevard, Los Angeles, CA 90034; 800/421-9194 (sales); 310/841-2790. *Fax:* 310/841-2559. *Price:* $39.95. *Platform:* Macintosh, MPC. *Grade Level:* Middle. *Curriculum:* Science.

A compilation of 70 video clips that looks at man's endeavors in areas of transportation, computation, tools, communication, time measurement, weapons and sensory extensions.

Interactive Storytime, Volumes 1 and 3. Interactive Publishing Corporation, 300 Airport Executive Park, Spring Valley, NY 10977; 800/472-8777 (orders); 914/426-0400. *Fax:* 914/426-2606. *Tech. Support:* 914/426-0400. *Price:* $49.95. *Platform:* Macintosh, DOS. *Grade Level:* Primary, Elementary. *Curriculum:* Storybook.

Each disk in the series contains several stories, with good animation and music. Each story can be printed out in black and white line drawings, as a coloring book.

Introductory Chemistry CD-ROM. Falcon Software, P.O. Box 200, Wentworth, NH 03282; 603/764-5788. *Fax:* 603/764-9051. *Tech. Support:* 617/235-1767. *Price:* $695. *Platform:* MPC. *Grade Level:* HS. *Curriculum:* Science.

Covers the laboratory, lecture and textbook topics of a first year general chemistry course. Includes over 200 interactive lessons, approximately 110 hours of instruction.

Journeys — Emergent Level One. *Operating System:* MAC. *Subject:* Literature. *Price:* $79. *Grade Level:* Ages 3 and up. *Hardware:* See distributor. *Software:* See distributor. *Distributor:* CD-ROM, Inc.

Variety of stories, poems, and songs with illustrations. The collection includes: *Fishing, I Like Rain, A House for a Mouse, Supper for a Troll, The Horrible Thing with Hairy Feet,* and *Stacks of Caps.*

Journeys — Emergent Level Two. *Operating System:* MAC. *Subject:* Literature and

Stories. *Price:* $79. *Grade Level:* Ages 3 and up. *Hardware:* See distributor. *Software:* See distributor. *Distributor:* CD-ROM, Inc.

Collection includes: *Are You There?, What Would You Like?, I'm a Prickly Crab, Who Will Be My Pet?, A Most Unusual Pet, An Animal Alphabet,* and *The Tiny Woman's Coat.*

Just Grandma and Me. *Operating System:* MAC. *Subject:* Literature. *Price:* $39. *Grade Level:* Ages 3 and up. *Hardware:* See distributor. *Software:* See distributor. *Distributor:* CD-ROM, Inc.

Story which is based on the best-selling book by Mercer Mayer, the award-winning author and illustrator. Little Critter takes a ride on a wind-blown umbrella, fends off a nasty crab, meets a variety of talented starfish and much, much more.

Kid's Zoo. Knowledge Adventure, 4502 Dyer Street, La Crescenta, CA 91214; 800/542-4240 (orders); 818/248-0166 (bulletin board). *Fax:* 818/542-4205. *Tech. Support:* 818/249-0212. *Price:* $79.95. *Platform:* DOS, Windows. *Grade Level:* Primary, Elementary. *Curriculum:* Science.

An introduction to the world of baby animals. Learn animal names, letter sounds, footprints, and what fur and feathers look like. Read along with a 30-page electronic book.

King James Bible. *Producer:* Bureau of Electronic Publishing. *Operating System:* PC. *Subject:* Religion. *Price:* $65. *Grade Level:* Elem., JH, HS. *Hardware:* See distributor. *Software:* See distributor. *Distributor:* Bureau of Electronic Publishing.

Search through the entire King James Bible, both the Old and New Testaments, completely indexed by words, chapter and verse.

Learn to Speak English. HyperGlot Software Co., Inc., P.O. Box 10746, Knoxville, TN 37939-0746; 800/949-4379; 615/558-8270. *Tech. Support:* 800/949-4379. *Price:* $99. *Platform:* Macintosh, MPC. *Grade Level:* JH, HS. *Curriculum:* Foreign Language.

Based on a course developed and used by the U.S. Foreign Service. A complete first year language course with extensive sound on two CDs. Thirty-six context-driven lessons with strong emphasis on understanding spoken language.

Learn to Speak French. HyperGlot Software Co., Inc., P.O. Box 10746, Knoxville, TN 37939-0746; 800/949-4379; 615/558-8270. *Fax:* 615/588-6569. *Tech. Support:* 800/949-4379. *Price:* $99. *Platform:* Macintosh, MPC. *Grade Level:* JH, HS. *Curriculum:* Foreign Language.

A complete first year language course with extensive sound on two CDs. Thirty-six context-driven lessons with strong emphasis on understanding spoken language.

Lenny's Music Toons. Paramount Interactive, 700 Hansen Way, Palo Alto, CA 94304; 415/813-8030. *Fax:* 415/813-8030. *Fax:* 415/813-8055. *Tech. Support:* 415/813-8030. *Price:* $39.95. *Platform:* Windows. *Grade Level:* Elementary. *Curriculum:* Arts and Music.

Meet Lenny, a world renowned musician, adventurer and collector of clever devices, who familiarizes children with music and exposes them to elements of music composition as well as sight reading and memory games.

Let's Go 1993 USA. Compton's NewMedia Inc., 2320 Camino Vida Roble, Carlsbad, CA 92009; 800/862-2206; 800/216-6116 (catalog sales); 619/929-2500. *Fax:* 619/929-2555. *Tech. Support:* 619/929-2626. *Price:* $24.95. *Platform:* Macintosh, DOS, MPC. *Grade Level:* JH, HS. *Curriculum:* Social Studies.

1993 — The Budget Guide to USA including Canada, Quebec, Ontario, British Columbia, and Yukon (maritime provinces).

Library of the Future Series. World Library Inc., 2809 Main Street, Irvine, CA 92714; 800/443-0238; 714/756-9500. *Fax:* 714/756-9511. *Tech. Support:* 714/756-9550. *Price:* $299. *Platform:* Macintosh, DOS, Windows. *Grade Level:* HS. *Curriculum:* Language Arts.

The complete text with illustrations of over 950 titles from over 500 works of literature, philosophy, drama, poetry, science and religion.

Lingua ROM 3. HyperGlot Software Co., Inc., P.O. Box 10746, Knoxville, TN 37939-0746; 800/949-4379; 615/558-8270. *Fax:* 615/588-6569. *Tech. Support:* 800/949-4379. *Price:* $999. *Platform:* Macintosh. *Grade Level:* HS. *Curriculum:* Foreign Language.

Complete interactive set for learning Chinese, French, German, Italian, Russian and Spanish.

A Long Hard Day on the Ranch. *Operating System:* MAC. *Subject:* Literature/Stories. *Price:* $69. *Grade Level:* Elem. *Hardware:* See distributor. *Software:* See distributor. *Distributor:* CD-ROM, Inc.

A little boy visits his uncle's farm and the story becomes a tall tale in a letter to his dad.

McGraw-Hill Science and Technical Reference Set. McGraw-Hill Inc., 11 W. 19th Street, New York NY 10011; 800/842-3075. *Fax:* 212/237-4092. *Tech. Support:* 800/551-2210. *Price:* $495. *Platform:* DOS. *Grade Level:* HS. *Curriculum:* Science.

Two standard references, the *Encyclopedia of Science and Technology*, 2nd edition, and the *Dictionary of Scientific and Technical Terms*, 4th edition.

Macnificent 7.0 Education and Tales. Wayzata Technology, 2515 East Highway 2, Grand Rapids, MI 55744; 800/377-7321; 218/326-0597; 218/326-2939 (bulletin board). *Fax:* 218/326-0598. *Tech. Support:* 800/377-7321. *Price:* $59. *Platform:* Macintosh. *Grade Level:* Elementary, Middle. *Curriculum:* Reference and Interdisciplinary.

Over 5,000 files, including System 7.1 games and educational shareware, plus commercial demos, sounds and sound stacks. Includes the Librarian, which provides searching access to all of this information. All files are indexed and described.

Magazine Article Summaries. *Producer:* EBSCO. *Subject:* Reference/Literature. *Price:* $99. *Grade Level:* JH, HS. *Hardware:* See distributor. *Software:* See distributor. *Distributor:* Bureau of Electronic Publishing.

Are you faced with the prospect of a semester's worth of reading in six hours — or just trying to understand the classics? For years, Simon & Schuster's "Monarch Notes" series have been a dream come true for students and parents. And with the release of the CD-ROM edition of the "Monarch Notes," the full text of the entire collection — over 200 different notes — are available for one low price. No more frantic trips around town searching for the notes you need, or last minute trips to the library. You can have the entire collection, many of which are no longer in print, for less than 50 cents per note (single copies can cost $5!).

Magazine Articles Summaries Select. EBSCO Publishing Inc., P.O. Box 2250,

Peabody, MA 01960-7250; 800/653-2726; 508/535-8500. *Fax:* 508/535-8545. *Tech. Support:* 808/758-5995. *Platform:* Macintosh, DOS. *Grade Level:* HS. *Curriculum:* Reference and Interdisciplinary.

Full text of 60 magazines plus indexing and abstracts from over 400 general magazines and the *New York Times.*

The Magic Flute. *Operating System:* MAC. *Subject:* Music. *Price:* $66. *Grade Level:* General. *Hardware:* See distributor. *Software:* See distributor. *Distributor:* Bureau of Electronic Publishing.

Mozart's opera *The Magic Flute,* conducted by Mikolaus Haroncourt, lets you see, hear and control a complete music program. *The Magic Flute* is playable on a CD player and contains the complete opera, on-screen commentary and annotation about the opera, and extra audio tracks to expand your understanding of the opera. It also contains a broad range of visual and audio information.

Magill's Survey of Science. EBSCO Publishing Inc., P.O. Box 2250, Peabody, MA 01960-7250; 800/653-2726; 508/535-8500. *Fax:* 508/535-8545. *Tech. Support:* 800/758-5995. *Price:* $895. *Platform:* DOS. *Grade Level:* HS. *Curriculum:* Science.

Magill's Survey of Science contains the complete text of four print reference series from Salem Press: *Earth Sciences,* 1990; *Life Science Series,* 1991; *Physical Science,* 1992; and *Applied Science Series,* 1993. Twenty-three volumes in total are included on the disk. Each volume in the series contains essays by various authors.

Mario's Early Years: Fun with Letters. The Software Toolworks Inc., 60 Leveroni Court, Novato, CA 94949; 800/231-3088; 415/883-3000. *Fax:* 415/883-3303. *Tech. Support:* 415/883-3000. *Price:* $49.95. *Platform:* DOS. *Grade Level:* Primary, Elementary. *Curriculum:* Language Arts.

Children discover the world around them by exploring the elements of that world. Children are introduced to the fundamentals of letters and sounds by way of learning worlds — Vowel, Alphabet, First Letter, Last Letter, Building, Blending and more.

Mars Explorer. Virtual Reality Labs Inc., 2341 Ganador Court, San Luis Obispo, CA 93401; 805/545-8515. *Fax:* 805/781-2259. *Tech. Support:* 805/545-8515. *Price:* $69.95. *Platform:* DOS. *Grade Level:* HS. *Curriculum:* Science.

A CD-ROM based program for viewing the surface of Mars, as photographed by NASA *Viking* orbiters. The program can overlay the IAU-approved names of objects of places as well as longitude and latitude lines with labels.

Math Finder. The Learning Team, 10 Long Pond Road, Armonk, NY 10504; 914/273-2226. *Fax:* 914/273-2227. *Price:* $295.99. *Platform:* Macintosh, DOS. *Grade Level:* Elem., JH, HS. *Curriculum:* Mathematics.

A computer access to curriculums to implement the NCTM Standards. Over 15,000 pages and 1,100 lessons of resources for math teachers to help in the curriculum development process.

Mathematics Vol. 1. Xploratorium, The Renaissance Project, Department of Education, Anglia Polytechnic, Sawyers Hall Lane, Brentwood, England CM15 9BT. *Price:* Write for information. *Platform:* Macintosh. *Grade Level:* HS. *Curriculum:* Mathematics.

Contains five sections (using Hypercard) — Numerical Analysis, Scientific and

Graphical Toolkit, HyperTest, Introduction to Calculus and Mathematical Modeling (Simple Harmonic Motion).

Mediasource — Historical Library Vol. 1. Applied Optical Media Corporation, 1450 Boot Road, Building 400A, West Chester, PA 19380; 800/321-7259; 610/429-3701. *Fax:* 610/429-3810. *Tech. Support:* 800/321-7259. *Price:* $395. *Platform:* Macintosh, MPC. *Grade Level:* HS. *Curriculum:* Arts and Music.

A collection of drawings, colored drawings and black and white photos of significant events and personalities from antiquity through WWII with a varied selection of background music fanfares and bridges and sound effects.

Mediasource — Natural Sciences Library Vol. I. Applied Optical Media Corporation, 1450 Boot Road, Building 400A, West Chester, PA 19380; 800/321-7259; 610/429-3701. *Fax:* 610/429-3810. *Tech. Support:* 800/321-7259. *Price:* $395. *Platform:* Macintosh, MPC. *Grade Level:* HS. *Curriculum:* Arts and Music.

A collection of full-color images on topics related to science including agriculture, anatomy, biology, botany, chemistry and physics, environment science, geology, nutrition, weather and climate and zoology with varied selection of background music fanfares.

Middle East Diary. Quanta Press Inc., 1313 Fifth Street, Suite SE 223A, Minneapolis, MN 55414; 612/379-3956. *Fax:* 612/623-4570. *Price:* $99.95. *Platform:* Macintosh, DOS. *Grade Level:* HS. *Curriculum:* Social Studies.

A lengthy review of Middle East history, personalities and conflicts. Includes travel, business and political information.

Middle Search. EBSCO Publishing Inc., P.O. Box 2250, Peabody, MA 01960-7250; 800/653-2726; 508/535-8500. *Fax:* 508/535-8545. *Tech. Support:* 800/758-5995. *Price:* 10×/yr., $899. *Platform:* Macintosh, DOS. *Grade Level:* JH, HS. *Curriculum:* Reference and Interdisciplinary.

Indexing and abstracts from 125 magazines, with full text from 33 magazines.

Mixed-Up Mother Goose. *Operating System:* PC. *Subject:* Literature/Reading. *Price:* $59. *Grade Level:* Elem., JH, HS. *Hardware:* See distributor. *Software:* See distributor. *Distributor:* Bureau of Electronic Publishing.

Mixed-Up Mother Goose is the best multimedia game we have ever seen for a PC. It combines animation, fascinating graphics, sound and text with a challenging game, all integrated into a pleasant, interactive story line designed for children four and up. It's so good that children of all ages will enjoy the game — and will be reluctant to leave this fairy land for the real world.

Monarch Notes. Two versions (network) available: For 2–9 stations: $295. For 10 or more stations: $595. Single: $79.95. (Also available with Chelsea House publishers: 1-800-848-BOOK.)

CD-ROM, full text. Bureau Development's Monarch Notes on CD-ROM contains information on the major works of more than 150 authors.

Movie Select. Paramount Interactive, 700 Hansen Way, Palo Alto, CA 94304; 415/813-8030. *Fax:* 415/813-8030. *Tech. Support:* 415/813-3030. *Price:* $39.95. *Platform:* Macintosh, MPC. *Grade Level:* JH, HS. *Curriculum:* Arts and Music.

A movie recommendation system to over 44,000 movies and videos.

Moving Gives Me a Stomach Ache. *Operating System:* MAC. *Subject:* Literature/Stories. *Price:* $84. *Grade Level:* Elem. *Hardware:* See distributor. *Software:* See distributor. *Distributor:* CD-ROM, Inc.
The story of a family in the process of moving told from the point of view of the little boy.

Mud Puddle. *Operating System:* MAC. *Subject:* Literature/Stories. *Price:* $74. *Grade Level:* Elem. *Hardware:* See distributor. *Software:* See distributor. *Distributor:* CD-ROM, Inc.
Keeping clean and tidy is a difficult job for any child, especially when a mud puddle is out to get you.

Multi-Bible CD-ROM. *Producer:* Innotech, Inc. *Operating System:* PC/MAC. *Subject:* Religion/Reference. *Price:* $130. *Grade Level:* General. *Hardware:* See distributor. *Software:* See distributor. *Distributor:* EBSCO.
This Bible CD-ROM contains a collection of Bible databases including Strong's Numbers, the Revised Standard Version, the New Revised Standard Version, the King James (authorized) Version, and the New King James Version.

Multimedia Audubon's Birds. Creative Multimedia, 514 NW 11th Avenue, Suite 203, Portland, OR 97209; 800/262-7668; 503/241-4351. *Fax:* 503/241-4370. *Tech. Support:* 503/241-1530. *Price:* $49.99. *Platform:* Macintosh, DOS. *Grade Level:* JH, HS. *Curriculum:* Science.
Full text of James Audubon's seven volume *Birds of America.* Birds of North America are included in 500 color plates, black and white figures and bird calls from library of Natural Sciences.

Multimedia Audubon's Mammals. Creative Multimedia, 514 NW 11th Avenue, Suite 203, Portland, OR 97209; 800/262-7668; 503/241-4351. *Fax:* 503/241-4370. *Tech. Support:* 503/241-1530. *Price:* $49.99. *Platform:* Macintosh, DOS. *Grade Level:* JH, HS. *Curriculum:* Science.
Contains the complete text of the 1840 first edition of "Octavio" set of John James Audubon's *Quadrupeds of North America.* Over 150 full-color mammal lithographs, full text indexing CD quality sounds for many mammals from Cornell Library of Natural Science.

Multimedia Business Week 1000 on CD-ROM. McGraw-Hill, Inc., 11 W. 19th Street, New York, NY 10011; 800/842-3075. *Fax:* 212/337-4092. *Tech. Support:* 800/551-2210. *Price:* $99. *Platform:* MPC. *Grade Level:* HS. *Curriculum:* Social Studies.
A profile of the *Business Week* 1,000 most valuable companies. Includes Standard and Poor's company data, 25 executives to watch, interviews with 13 top executives and multimedia essay.

Multimedia Encyclopedia of Mammalian Biology. McGraw-Hill Inc., 11 W. 19th Street, New York, NY 10011; 800/842-3075. *Fax:* 212/337-4092. *Tech. Support:* 800/551-2210. *Price:* $495. *Platform:* Windows. *Grade Level:* HS. *Curriculum:* Science.
The full-text color photographs, artwork and maps of all five volumes of Grzimek's *Encyclopedia of Mammals.* Includes 3,500 full-color images and 500 maps, full glossary of terms, full current bibliography of scientific literature, and movie and sound.

Multimedia Family Bible. Candlelight Publishing, P.O. Box 5213, Mesa, AZ 85211-5213; 800/677-3045. *Fax:* 801/373-2499. *Tech. Support:* 800/677-3045. *Price:* $39.95. *Platform:* Windows. *Grade Level:* HS. *Curriculum:* Reference and Interdisciplinary.

Combines the classic King James text with 44 animated Bible stories, detailed full-color maps and gazetteer of the Holy Land, more than 100 photos of significant sites in the Holy Land, and a fully linked Greek and Hebrew lexicon.

Multimedia Music Book: Mozart. Ebook Inc., 23970 Alvarado-Niles Road, Suite 704, Union City, CA 94587; 510/429-1331. *Fax:* 510/429-1394. *Tech. Support:* 510/713-8904. *Price:* $24.95. *Platform:* Macintosh, MPC. *Grade Level:* HS. *Curriculum:* Arts and Music.

Provides information on the composer's music and life.

Multimedia U.S. History. *Operating System:* Windows. *Subject:* U.S. History. *Grade Level:* General. *Hardware:* See distributor. *Software:* See distributor. *Distributor:* Updata.

Track the evolution of the United States from Columbus' first explorations through today.

Multimedia World Fact Book and CIA World Tour. *Operating System:* PC/MAC/MPC. *Subject:* Reference. *Price:* $99. *Grade Level:* JH, HS. *Hardware:* See distributor. *Software:* See distributor. *Distributor:* Bureau of Electronic Publishing.

Whether you're planning a coup in a South American dictatorship or just checking the terrain in Tehran for a tête-à-tête, the CIA has the information you need. Included are 248 comprehensive country profiles.

Multimedia World Factbook. Bureau for Electronic Publishing, 141 New Road, Parsippany, NJ 07054; 800/828-4766 (orders); 201/808-2700. *Fax:* 201/808-2676. *Tech. Support:* 201/808-2700, Ext. 22. *Price:* $29.95. *Platform:* Macintosh, DOS, MPC. *Grade Level:* HS. *Curriculum:* Social Studies.

Contains 248 country profiles from the CIA yearbook, with added information from the KGB yearbook, Hammond maps and segments of national anthems.

My Advanced Label Designer. My Software Company, 1259 El Camino Real, Suite 167, Menlo Park, CA 94025; 800/325-3508 (orders); 415/325-4222. *Price:* $59.95. *Platform:* Macintosh, Windows. *Grade Level:* JH, HS. *Curriculum:* General.

Labels are professionally designed by importing your own company graphics or select from dozens of clip art images.

The Myths and Legends of Ancient Greece. *Operating Systems:* DOS, MAC, Windows. *Subject:* History. *Grade Level:* General. *Hardware:* See distributor. *Software:* See distributor. *Distributor:* Updata.

Learn the stories of the ten best-known Greek myths. Contains an audio-visual presentation with text linked to a 24-volume student encyclopedia and glossary.

National Directory. *Operating System:* MAC. *Subject:* Reference. *Price:* $195. *Grade Level:* General. *Hardware:* See distributor. *Software:* See distributor. *Distributor:* Bureau of Electronic Publishing.

A comprehensive listing of the most useful and important addresses, telephone, fax and telex numbers in the United States and the world — 120,000 entries. Users can automatically dial or fax numbers, print lists, and export to other programs.

National Parks: The Multimedia Family Guide. Cambrix Publishing, 6269 Variel Avenue, Suite B, Woodland Hills, CA 91367; 818/992-8484. *Fax:* 818/992-8781. *Tech. Support:* 818/992-8484. *Price:* $59.95. *Platform:* Macintosh, MPC. *Grade Level:* JH, HS. *Curriculum:* Reference and Interdisciplinary.

A comprehensive interactive directory of all the National Parks of America. Includes videos, photographs, travel planning, and searching park index.

National Parks: The Multimedia Family Guide. *Operating System:* Windows. *Subject:* Travel. *Grade Level:* General. *Hardware:* See distributor. *Software:* See distributor. *Distributor:* Updata.

Contains over 40 videos, 400 photographs, audio and numerous information screens on all national parks, monuments, memorials, battlefields, etc.

National Parks of America. *Operating Systems:* MAC, MPC. *Subject:* National parks. *Grade Level:* General. *Hardware:* See distributor. *Software:* See distributor. *Distributor:* Updata.

Contains more than 900 breathtaking photographs of America's national parks. Research park background information and climate conditions.

Nautilus. Metatec Corporation, 7001 Metatec Boulevard, Dublin, OH 43017; 614/761-2000. *Fax:* 614/761-4258. *Tech. Support:* 614/766-3150. *Price:* $137.40, 12 monthly issues. *Platform:* Macintosh, Windows. *Grade Level:* HS. *Curriculum:* Reference and Interdisciplinary.

A multimedia magazine on CD-ROM that provides information and software for Macintosh and DOS users.

New Basics Electronic Cookbook. XIPHIAS, 8758 Venice Boulevard, Los Angeles, CA 90034; 800/421-9194 (sales); 310/841-2790. *Fax:* 310/841-2559. *Price:* $69.95. *Platform:* DOS, MPC. *Grade Level:* HS. *Curriculum:* Reference and Interdisciplinary.

Created from *Silver Palate Cookbook* series by the authors Julie Rosso and Sheila Likins. Includes a library of over 1,800 recipes, hundreds of color pictures, and cooking hints.

New York Times Ondisc. University Microfilm International, 300 North Zeeb Road, Ann Arbor, MI 48106; 313/761-4700. *Fax:* 313/761-1204. *Tech. Support:* 800/521-0600, Ext. 2513. *Price:* $2450. *Platform:* DOS. *Grade Level:* HS. *Curriculum:* Reference and Interdisciplinary.

Contains all the articles in full text published from 1990 to the present. Updated monthly.

Newsbank CD Junior. NewsBank, Inc., 58 Pine Street, New Canaan, CT 06840-5426; 800/762-8182; 203/966-1103. *Fax:* 203/966-6254. *Tech. Support:* 800/762-8182. *Price:* $795. *Platform:* DOS. *Grade Level:* Middle. *Curriculum:* Reference and Interdisciplinary.

Citations from over 105 magazines with 10 magazines full text, plus articles from 40 newspapers.

Newsbank Index to Periodicals. NewsBank, Inc., 58 Pine Street, New Canaan, CT

06840-5426; 800/762-8182; 203/966-1100. *Fax:* 203/966-6254. *Tech. Support:* 800/762-8182. *Platform:* DOS. *Grade Level:* JH, HS. *Curriculum:* Reference and Interdisciplinary.

Citations from over 200 magazines from 1988 to the present. Includes abstract and full bibliographic data.

Newsweek Interactive — Unfinished Business. The Software Toolworks Inc., 60 Leveroni Court, Novato, CA 94949; 800/231-3088; 415/883-3000. *Fax:* 415/883-3303. *Tech. Support:* 415/883-3000. *Price:* $129.95, four editions. *Platform:* DOS. *Grade Level:* Senior High School. *Curriculum:* Social Studies.

An interactive disk covering current events through *Newsweek* correspondents.

The Night Before Christmas. *Operating System:* MAC. *Subject:* Literature. *Price:* $69. *Grade Level:* K–Elem. *Hardware:* See distributor. *Software:* See distributor. *Distributor:* CD-ROM, Inc.

This is a classic that both adults and children enjoy. Tale with Arthur Rackham illustrations. Keyboard skills are not needed, only ability to "point and click."

North American Indians. *Operating Systems:* DOS, MAC. *Subject:* Native Americans. *Grade Level:* General. *Hardware:* See distributor. *Software:* See distributor. *Distributor:* Updata.

Text and images on the history of Native Americans. The database includes information on leadership, tribal heritage, religion, family life, customs, wars, weaponry, art and artifacts, reservations and resettlement.

North American Indians. Quanta Press Inc., 1313 Fifth Street, Suite SE 223A, Minneapolis, MN 55414; 612/379-3956. *Fax:* 612/623-4570. *Price:* $69.95. *Platform:* Macintosh, DOS. *Grade Level:* HS. *Curriculum:* Social Studies.

North American Indians CD includes original information about the American Indian with historical photographs and interpretations.

Oxford Shakespeare. *Operating Systems:* MAC, Windows. *Subject:* English Literature. *Grade Level:* General. *Hardware:* See distributor. *Software:* See distributor. *Distributor:* Updata.

Features animated graphical interface and search facility of all titles and texts of Shakespeare's works. The complete texts are also in an integral word processing application, allowing you to alter, edit and print any of Shakespeare's work.

Oxford Textbook of Medicine. *Operating System:* DOS. *Subject:* Internal Medicine. *Grade Level:* General. *Hardware:* See distributor. *Software:* See distributor. *Distributor:* Updata.

Able to access the most comprehensive and up-to-date textbook to cover the entire range of internal medicine on CD-ROM.

PC Globe Maps 'n' Facts. *Operating System:* DOS. *Subject:* World Atlas. *Grade Level:* General. *Hardware:* See distributor. *Software:* See distributor. *Distributor:* Updata.

This comprehensive, versatile resource gives access to detailed maps of and vast amounts of information on countries around the world.

Peter and the Wolf. Ebook Inc., 32970 Alvarado-Niles Road, Suite 704, Union City, CA 94587; 510/429-1331. *Fax:* 510/429-1394. *Tech. Support:* 510/713-8904.

Price: $34.95. *Platform:* Macintosh, MPC. *Grade Level:* Middle. *Curriculum:* Language Arts.

Prokofiev's famous musical piece, narrated by Jack Lemmon, with pictures and musical surprises. Can also be listened to on a standard CD-audio player.

Peterson's College Database. SilverPlatter Information Inc., 100 River Ridge Drive, Norwood, MA 02062-5026; 800/343-0064; 617/679-2599. *Fax:* 617/769-8763. *Tech. Support:* 800/343-0064. *Price:* $595, single user; $995, 8 network users. *Platform:* DOS. *Grade Level:* HS. *Curriculum:* Reference and Interdisciplinary.

Individual descriptive profiles of 3,300 accredited degree-granting colleges. Includes statistics, expenses, financial aid, majors offered, and more.

Photo Pro. Wayzata Technologies, 2515 East Highway 2, Grand Rapids, MI 55744; 800/377-7321; 218/326-0597; 218/326-2939 (bulletin board). *Fax:* 218/326-0598. *Tech. Support:* 800/377-7321. *Price:* $129. *Platform:* DOS. *Grade Level:* HS. *Curriculum:* Arts and Music.

A collection of over 100 photographs of nature scenes taken in the Midwest USA. Format is 24-bit TIFF and PCX. Full reproduction rights for users.

Physician's Desk Reference. Medical Economics Data, 5 Paragon Drive, Montvale, NJ 07645, 201/358-7200. *Fax:* 201/573-0867. *Price:* $595, includes two updates. *Platform:* DOS. *Grade Level:* HS. *Curriculum:* Health.

A 2,000 page comprehensive pharmaceutical reference system, which contains a complete collection of prescribing references published by PDR including all product descriptions, *Physician's Desk Reference, PDR for Ophthalmology,* and *PDR for Nonprescription Drugs.*

Pilgrim Quest. Decision Development Corp., 2680 Bishop Drive, Suite 122, San Ramon, CA 94583; 800/835-4332. *Fax:* 510/830-0830. *Tech. Support:* 800/835-4332. *Price:* $99.95; school, $129.95. *Platform:* DOS. *Grade Level:* Elem., JH, HS. *Curriculum:* Social Studies.

Challenges students with choices and situations like those the Pilgrims faced. School version includes lesson plans, teacher's guide and audio cassette.

Pixel Garden. Quanta Press, Inc., 1313 Fifth Street, Suite SE 223A, Minneapolis, MN 55414; 612/379-3956. *Fax:* 612/623-4570. *Price:* $79.95. *Platform:* DOS. *Grade Level:* HS. *Curriculum:* Science.

Database of 522 ornamental plants common in the United States. Includes color photograph (560 images) and specific attributes.

Planet Earth: Gaia Library. Xploratorium, The Renaissance Project, Department of Education, Anglia Polytechnic, Sawyers Hall Lane, Brentwood, England CM15 9BT. *Platform:* Macintosh. *Grade Level:* Senior High School. *Curriculum:* Science.

Uses James Lovelock's Gaia Theory, Stella simulations of Daisyworlds, resources and learning activities to advance the idea that life on earth is a self-modifying and self-regulating system. Includes environmental studies, geology and oceanography.

The Plant Doctor. Quanta Press Inc., 1313 Fifth Street, Suite SE 223A, Minneapolis, MN 55414; 612/379-3956. *Fax:* 612/623-4570. *Price:* $49.95. *Platform:* Macintosh, DOS. *Grade Level:* HS. *Curriculum:* Science.

A multimedia database on trees, turf, flowers, shrubs and other plants along with plant disorders and cures.

Poem Finder on Disc. *Operating Systems:* DOS, Windows. *Subject:* Poetry. *Grade Level:* General. *Hardware:* See distributor. *Software:* See distributor. *Distributor:* Updata.

This comprehensive index of over 440,000 English-language poems ranges from the traditional to the most contemporary. Every citation provides full bibliographic information for the poem source including page numbers.

Poem Finder. Roth Publishing, 185 Great Neck Road, Great Neck, NY 11021; 800/899-7684. *Fax:* 516/829-7746. *Tech. Support:* 800/899-7684. *Price:* $39.95. *Platform:* DOS. *Grade Level:* HS. *Curriculum:* Language Arts.

Indexes 270,000 poems in 1,322 anthologies, 1,300 single author collections and over 100 periodicals. Keyword searching through all fields, author, translator, poem, title, book or periodical title first line. All citations provide full bibliographical information.

Portraits of American Presidents. *Operating System:* Windows. *Subject:* History. *Grade Level:* General. *Hardware:* See distributor. *Software:* See distributor. *Distributor:* Updata.

Browse through more than 200 years of our nation's presidents from George Washington to Bill Clinton. Features historic news video clips, live presidential recordings, rare archival photographs and illustrations.

Prescription Drugs: A Pharmacist's Guide. Quanta Press Inc., 1313 Fifth Street, Suite SE 223A, Minneapolis, MN 55414; 612/379-3956. *Fax:* 612/623-4570. *Price:* $79.95. *Platform:* Macintosh, DOS, Windows. *Grade Level:* HS. *Curriculum:* Health.

A pharmacist's guide compiling several health professional references translated into everyday language. Most commonly used drugs are listed with remarks on doses, side effects and how each drug works in the body.

The Presidents: A Picture History of Our Nation. *Operating System:* DOS. *Subject:* Presidents of the U.S. *Grade Level:* JH to Adult. *Hardware:* See distributor. *Software:* See distributor. *Distributor:* Updata.

Discover the personal and political lives, careers, campaign, and the social and historical times of each of our presidents.

Primary Search. EBSCO Publishing Inc., P.O. Box 2250, Peabody, MA 01960-7250; 800/653-2726; 508/535-8500. *Fax:* 508/535-8545. *Tech. Support:* 800/758-5995. *Price:* 3 discs, $549. *Platform:* Macintosh, DOS. *Grade Level:* Elementary, Middle. *Curriculum:* Reference and Interdisciplinary.

Indexing and abstracts from 90 magazines. Full text from 10 magazines. Includes some images and is keyword searchable.

Proart. Multi-Ad Services Inc., 1720 W. Detweiler Drive, Peoria, IL 61615-1695; 309/692-1530. *Fax:* 309/692-6566. *Price:* $32. *Platform:* Macintosh, DOS. *Grade Level:* HS. *Curriculum:* Arts and Music.

Over 300 high quality clip art illustrations which can be imported into many applications.

Professional Tutor: Learning Windows. Paragon Consultants Inc., 158 Sandy Drive, Boulder, CO 80302; 303/442-1613. *Fax:* 303/939-0290. *Tech. Support:* 303/465-0195. *Price:* $39.95. *Platform:* MPC. *Grade Level:* HS. *Curriculum:* General.
A step-by-step introduction to Windows.

Project Gutenberg. Walnut Creek CDROM, 1547 Palos Verdes Mall #260, Walnut Creek, CA 94596; 800/786-9907; 510/674-0783. *Price:* $39.95. *Platform:* Macintosh. *Grade Level:* HS. *Curriculum:* Language Arts.
ISO-9660 ASCII text CD-ROM. Contains full text of 1991–93 text project, which includes classic literature, source documents, religious text, census data, CIA World Fact Book, almanacs, etc.

Quick Art Lite. Wayzata Technologies, 2515 East Highway 2, Grand Rapids, MI 55744; 800/377-7321; 218/326-0597; 218/326-2939 (bulletin board). *Fax:* 218/326-0598. *Tech. Support:* 800/377-7321. *Price:* $119. *Platform:* Macintosh, DOS. *Grade Level:* HS. *Curriculum:* Arts and Music.
Professionally drawn, top quality (300dpi); images used for desktop publishing, brochures, ads, reports and catalogs. Includes over 3,300 images.

Readers' Guide Abstracts, Select Edition. H.W. Wilson Company, 950 University Avenue, Bronx, NY 10452; 800/367-6770; 718/588-8400. *Fax:* 718/590-1617. *Tech. Support:* 800/367-6770, Ext. 6004. *Platform:* DOS. *Price:* 4×/yr., $395; 10×/yr., $695; 12×/yr., $995. *Grade Level:* JH, HS. *Curriculum:* Reference and Interdisciplinary.
Indexes 240 periodicals and the *New York Times*, from 1983 to the present. Includes enhanced titles and subject headings.

Readers' Guide to Periodical Literature. H.W. Wilson Company, 950 University Avenue, Bronx, NY 10452; 800/367-6770; 718/588-8400. *Fax:* 715/590-1617. *Tech. Support:* 800/367-6770, Ext. 6004. *Platform:* DOS. *Price:* 12×/yr., $825. *Grade Level:* JH, HS. *Curriculum:* Reference and Interdisciplinary.
Indexes 240 periodicals and the *New York Times*, from 1983 to the present. Includes enhanced titles and subject headings.

The Reading Carnival. Digital Theater, 5875 Peachtree Industrial Boulevard, Suite 150, Norcross, GA 30092; 800/344-8246 (orders); 404/446-3580. *Fax:* 404/446-9164. *Tech. Support:* 404/446-3337. *Price:* $49.95; school, $69.95. *Grade Level:* Primary, Elementary. *Curriculum:* Language Arts.
Through the use of color and music, children become involved in reading and learning. Children explore sections on Animal Facts, Super Hero Stories and Fascinating Facts to encourage natural inquisitiveness.

Reading Short Stories. *Producer:* Queue. *Operating System:* PC. *Subject:* Reading. *Price:* $95. *Grade Level:* Elem., JH. *Hardware:* See distributor. *Software:* See distributor. *Distributor:* CDiscovery.
Contains the complete Reading and Interpreting Literature Series from Intellectual Software plus some of the world's greatest short stories and uses them as the basis for interesting, educational tutorials in reading comprehension. The stories, such as *Aesop's Fables, The Emperor's New Clothes, The Ugly Duckling, The Princess and the Pea, The Gift of the Magi, Make Westing, The Tell-Tale Heart, Rumpelstiltskin, Brave Little*

Tailor, and *The Lady or the Tiger* are presented with passages that are read at a student's own pace. Then, with the story still on screen, it reinforces comprehension as well as critical reading and evaluative thinking skills. Wrong answers result in hints, and, after a second try, feedback is provided in the form of the passage which contains the answer.

Scary Poems for Rotten Kids. *Operating System:* MAC. *Subject:* Literature/Poetry. *Price:* $84. *Grade Level:* Elem. *Hardware:* See distributor. *Software:* See distributor. *Distributor:* CD-ROM, Inc.
　　Children today live with the same fears we all had as children.

Science Helper K–8. The Learning Team, 10 Long Pond Road, Armonk, NY 10504; 914/273-2226. *Fax:* 914/273-2227. *Price:* $195. *Platform:* Macintosh, DOS. *Grade Level:* Primary, Elementary, Middle. *Curriculum:* Science.
　　Science helper includes plans for 1,000 hands-on science lessons from six full elementary science programs developed over a 15-year period by hundreds of teachers.

Shakespeare. Creative Multimedia, 514 NW 11th Avenue, Suite 203, Portland, OR 97209; 800/262-7668; 503/241-4351. *Fax:* 503/241-4370. *Tech. Support:* 503/241-1530. *Price:* $29.99. *Platform:* Macintosh, DOS. *Grade Level:* HS. *Curriculum:* Language Arts.
　　The complete works of William Shakespeare.

Sherlock Holmes: Consulting Detective Vol. 3. VIACOM NewMedia Inc., 648 S. Wheeling Road, Wheeling, IL 60090; 708/520-4440. *Fax:* 708/459-7456. *Price:* $49.95, vol. 1 and 2; $69.95, vol. 3. *Platform:* Macintosh, DOS. *Grade Level:* HS. *Curriculum:* Language Arts.
　　Three full-motion, color video detective stories based on classic Sherlock Holmes cases are on each disk. A user can interact with each story, collect clues and help solve the case.

Sherlock Holmes on Disc. Creative Multimedia, 514 NW 11th Avenue, Suite 203, Portland, OR 97209; 800/262-7668; 503/241-4351. *Fax:* 503/241-4370. *Tech. Support:* 503/241-1530. *Price:* $29.99. *Platform:* Macintosh, DOS. *Grade Level:* Senior High School. *Curriculum:* Language Arts.
　　The complete text of all Sherlock Holmes stories by Sir Arthur Conan Doyle as well as *The Medical Casebook* of Dr. Arthur Conan Doyle, *Linoleum Block Prints* by Dr. George Wells, and *Medical Poetry* by Dr. George Bascom.

A Silly, Noisy House. *Operating System:* MAC. *Subject:* Reading. *Price:* $59. *Grade Level:* K. *Hardware:* See distributor. *Software:* See distributor. *Distributor:* CDiscovery.
　　Children explore the rooms of a bright and cheery home, pointing, clicking, and discovering hidden surprises like secret passageways, birthday parties, magic wands and piano-playing spiders! This animated audio toybox also contains over 250 sound effects, songs, and rhymes. Introduces children ages three and over to Macintosh and the world of computers. This disk requires no reading.

The Sleeping Beauty. Ebook Inc., 32970 Alvarado-Niles Road, Suite 704, Union City, CA 94587; 510/429-1331. *Fax:* 510/429-1394. *Tech. Support:* 510/713-8904. *Price:* $34.95. *Platform:* MPC. *Grade Level:* Elementary. *Curriculum:* Language Arts.

A world of make believe kings and queens, princesses, witches and a hundred-year spell. With a combination of animation, art and music, you enjoy a fascinating array of moving pictures.

The Software Toolworks Illustrated Encyclopedia. The Software Toolworks Inc., 60 Leveroni Court, Novato, CA 94949; 800/231-3088; 415/883-3000. *Fax:* 415/883-3303. *Tech. Support:* 415/883-3000. *Price:* $395. *Grade Level:* JH, HS. *Curriculum:* Reference and Interdisciplinary.

More than 33,000 articles with numerous full-color illustrations and photos. CD-audio capabilities offer high-quality sound, including musical instruments, animal sounds, as well as recordings of historical and political figures.

The Software Toolworks 20th Century Video Almanac. The Software Toolworks, Inc., 60 Leveroni Court, Novato, CA 94949; 800/231-3088; 415/883-3000. *Fax:* 415/883-3303. *Tech. Support:* 415/883-3000. *Price:* $69.95; five disc set, $199.95. *Platform:* Macintosh, DOS, Windows. *Grade Level:* JH, HS. *Curriculum:* Social Studies.

A multimedia reference work that uses an extensive archive of motion videos to produce a visual encyclopedia of the century. Listen to President Kennedy, attend Woodstock, and land on the moon. Also includes text, audio and photographs.

Space: A Visual History of Manned Spaceflight. Sumeria, 329 Bryant Street, Suite 3D; San Francisco, CA 94107; 415/904-0800. *Fax:* 415/904-0888. *Tech. Support:* 415/904-0800. *Price:* $49.95. *Platform:* Macintosh, Windows. *Grade Level:* JH, HS. *Curriculum:* Science.

Based on NASA film archives, shows all manned space flights from Mercury in 1949 to the present-day shuttle flights. Includes topics on space technology, such as space suits and life in space.

Space Adventure. Knowledge Adventure, 4502 Dyer Street, La Crescenta, CA 91214; 800/542-4240 (orders); 818/248-0166 (bulletin board). *Fax:* 818/542-4205. *Tech. Support:* 818/249-0212. *Price:* $79.95. *Platform:* DOS. *Grade Level:* JH, HS. *Curriculum:* Science.

A journey into space that takes you past hundreds of breathtaking views, realistic sounds, and musical accompaniment. Simulations with informative note balloons and text will open your mind to the mysteries of space.

Space Series — Apollo. Quanta Press Inc., 1313 Fifth Street, Suite SE 223A, Minneapolis, MN 55414; 612/379-3956. *Fax:* 612/623-4570. *Price:* $69.95. *Platform:* Macintosh, DOS. *Grade Level:* HS. *Curriculum:* Science.

Over 200 color, black and white photographs and a collection of full-text documents from NASA plus interviews with members of the space program. Chronology from rocket pioneering in 1920 to *Apollo* 18 splashdown.

Space Time and Art. Wayzata Technologies, 2515 East Highway 2, Grand Rapids, MI 55774; 800/377-7321; 218/326-0597; 218/326-2939 (bulletin board). *Fax:* 218/326-0598. *Tech. Support:* 800/377-7321. *Price:* $199. *Platform:* Macintosh. *Grade Level:* HS. *Curriculum:* Arts and Music.

Short demonstration movie clips and animations illustrating recent theories of creation in the cosmos. Four files discuss various aspects of cosmological theory and how they influence art. Dimensions of space, questions of time, space time and the arts.

Sports Illustrated CD-ROM Sports Almanac. Time Warner Interactive Group, 2210 West Olive Avenue, Burbank, CA 91506-2626; 800/593-6334; 818/955-9999. *Fax:* 818/955-6499. *Tech. Support:* 800/565-TWIG. *Price:* $59.99. *Platform:* Macintosh, DOS. *Grade Level:* JH, HS. *Curriculum:* Sports.

Dozens of articles by top sports writers, a chronological listing of 199 sports highlights, profiles of 500 prominent names in sports, and athletic awards from 1931 to the present.

Story Time. Houghton Mifflin, 222 Berkeley Street, Boston, MA 02116-3764; 617/351-5000. *Fax:* 617/351-1100. *Tech. Support:* 800/758-6762. *Price:* ABC, $95; Level 1, $426; Level 2, $426; 2+, $528; 2+2+, $894; complete set, $1950. *Platform:* Macintosh. *Grade Level:* Primary, Elementary. *Curriculum:* Storybook.

A children's reading program centered on themes each offering three activities centers — reading, writing and story support. Supports English and Spanish.

Street Atlas USA. *Operating System:* PC. *Subject:* Reference. *Price:* $95. *Grade Level:* General. *Hardware:* IBM/Compatible. *Software:* See distributor. *Distributor:* Bureau of Electronic Publishing.

Detailed, street level maps of every street in the United States (including their names) on one disk. Locations by street name, phone exchange, zip code, or place name. Displays street addresses and city blocks in metropolitan areas. Windows required.

Super Tom. Information Access Company, 362 Lakeside Drive, Foster City, CA 94404; 800/227-8431; 415/378-5200. *Fax:* 415/358-4769. *Tech. Support:* 800/227-8431. *Price:* N/A. *Platform:* DOS. *Grade Level:* HS. *Curriculum:* Reference and Interdisciplinary.

Indexes 180+ magazines, 100 are full-text; includes selected full-text newspaper articles and four reference books.

Super Tom Junior. Information Access Company, 362 Lakeside Drive, Foster City, CA 94404; 800/227-8431; 415/378-5200. *Fax:* 415/358-4769. *Tech. Support:* 800/227-8431. *Price:* N/A. *Platform:* DOS. *Grade Level:* Middle. *Curriculum:* Reference and Interdisciplinary.

Indexes 55 magazines, 38 are full-text, plus selected full-text newspaper articles and four reference books.

Survey of Western Art. Ebook Inc., 32970 Alvarado-Niles Road, Suite 704, Union City, CA 94587; 510/429-1331. *Fax:* 510/429-1394. *Tech. Support:* 510/713-8904. *Price:* $49.95. *Platform:* Macintosh, MPC, DOS. *Grade Level:* HS. *Curriculum:* Arts and Music.

Over 1,000 full-color fine print art images, with accompanying text and explanations.

The Tale of Benjamin Bunny. *Operating System:* MAC. *Subject:* Literature/Stories. *Price:* $69. *Grade Level:* Elem. *Hardware:* See distributor. *Software:* See distributor. *Distributor:* CD-ROM, Inc.

Peter Rabbit and his cousin Benjamin Bunny set out to retrieve Peter's clothes.

The Tale of Peter Rabbit. Knowledge Adventure 4502 Dyer Street, La Crescenta, CA 91214; 800/542-4240 (orders); 818/248-0166 (bulletin board). *Fax:* 818/542-4205. *Tech. Support:* 818/249-0212. *Price:* $22.48. *Platform:* DOS. *Grade Level:* Primary, Elementary. *Curriculum:* Language Arts.

Taken from the classic Beatrix Potter text with illustrations by L. Johnson to create original water colors for this talking storybook. Characters can be activated on the screen, and children learn to spell and pronounce words.

Talking Classic Tales. New Media Schoolhouse, Box 390, 69 Westchester Avenue, Pound Ridge, NY 10576; 800/672-6002. *Fax:* 914/764-0104. *Tech. Support:* 800/672-6002. *Price:* $89. *Grade Level:* Primary. *Curriculum:* Storybook.

Five classic stories, like *Puss-in-Boots* and *Rumpelstiltskin*, to listen to or to read.

Talking Jungle Safari. New Media Schoolhouse, Box 390, 69 Westchester Avenue, Pound Ridge, NY 10576; 800/672-6002. *Fax:* 914/764-0104. *Tech. Support:* 800/672-6002. *Price:* $79. *Grade Level:* Primary, Elementary. *Curriculum:* Science.

Interactive trip through the African jungle; learn about animals, habitats and ecosystems.

Tao of Cow. Quanta Press Inc., 1313 Fifth Street, Suite SE 223A, Minneapolis, MN 55414; 612/379-3946. *Fax:* 612/623-4570. *Price:* $29.95. *Platform:* Macintosh, DOS. *Grade Level:* JH, HS. *Curriculum:* Social Studies.

Hundreds of black and white and full-color photographs of cows, along with short Zen-like statements about cows.

Thomas' Snowsuit. *Operating System:* MAC. *Subject:* Literature/Stories. *Price:* $74. *Grade Level:* Elem. *Hardware:* See distributor. *Software:* See distributor. *Distributor:* CD-ROM, Inc.

Shows the frustration of adults and children alike during snowsuit weather.

Three-D Dinosaur. Knowledge Adventure, 4502 Dyer Street, La Crescenta, CA 91214; 800/542-4240 (orders); 818/248-0166 (bulletin board). *Fax:* 818/542-4205. *Tech. Support:* 818/249-0212. *Price:* $79.98. *Platform:* DOS, Windows. *Grade Level:* Elementary, Middle. *Curriculum:* Science.

Don your 3-D glasses to see dinosaurs come right out of your computer screen, watch 30 movies, design your own dino, or check out 150 million years' worth of paleontological findings.

Time Table of History: Arts and Entertainment. XIPHIAS, 8758 Venice Boulevard, Los Angeles, CA 90034; 800/421-9194 (sales); 310/841-2790. *Fax:* 310/841-2559. *Price:* $59.95. *Platform:* DOS, MPC. *Grade Level:* JH, HS. *Curriculum:* Arts and Music.

History of 4,000 stories linked to efforts including graphics and maps, pictures, quotes, sounds, music, etc. Also topics from the first cave paintings to computer generated choreography.

Time Table of History: Business Politics and Media. XIPHIAS, 8758 Venice Boulevard, Los Angeles, CA 90034; 800/421-9194 (sales); 310/841-2790. *Fax:* 310/841-2559. *Price:* $59.95. *Platform:* DOS, MPC. *Grade Level:* JH, HS. *Curriculum:* Social Studies.

Six thousand stories enriched by images, maps, sounds and more. From the Trojan horse to Desert Storm, the quest for wealth, power and knowledge is richly illustrated in this interactive environment.

Time Table of History: Science and Innovation. XIPHIAS, 8758 Venice Boulevard, Los Angeles, CA 90034; 800/421-9194 (sales); 310/841-2790. *Fax:* 310/841-2559. *Price:* $59.95. *Platform:* DOS, MPC. *Grade Level:* JH, HS. *Curriculum:* Science.

The way to learn about man's progress in science and development of technology. Over 6,300 stories linked to special effects, including maps, pictures, sounds, prehistoric timelines, etc. Arranged chronologically from the first stirring of life on the planet to the present world of high technology.

Tom Health and Science. *Producer:* Information Access. *Operating System:* PC/MAC. *Subject:* Reference. *Price:* $1,100—annual subscription. *Grade Level:* General. *Hardware:* See distributor. *Software:* See distributor. *Distributor:* Information Access.

Provides access to articles from more than 50 publications in the health and science field. Very easy to access information.

Tom Junior. Information Access Company, 362 Lakeside Drive, Foster City, CA 94404; 800/227-8431; 415/378-5200. *Fax:* 415/358-4769. *Tech. Support:* 800/227-8431. *Price:* $800. *Platform:* DOS. *Grade Level:* JH, HS. *Curriculum:* Reference and Interdisciplinary.

Indexes 55 magazines; 38 are full-text.

Toolworks Mac. *Operating System:* MAC. *Subject:* Reference. *Price:* $649. *Grade Level:* General: *Hardware:* See distributor. *Software:* See distributor. *Distributor:* CDiscovery.

Everything you need to get started: *Illustrated Encyclopedia, Time Table of History, U.S. History, CD Funhouse.*

Toolworks Reference Library. *Operating System:* PC. *Subject:* Reference. *Price:* $149. *Grade Level:* K–C. *Hardware:* IBM PC. *Software:* See distributor. *Distributor:* CDiscovery.

Includes *The New York Public Library Desk Reference, Webster's New World Thesaurus, Webster's New World Guide to Concise Writing, Webster's New World Dictionary Third College Edition, The Dictionary of 20th Century History, J.K. Lasser's Legal and Corporation Forms for the Smaller Business, Webster's New World Dictionary of Quotable Definitions* and *The National Directory of Addresses and Telephone Numbers.*

Total Baseball. Creative Multimedia, 514 NW 11th Avenue, Suite 203, Portland, OR 97209; 800/262-7668; 503/241-4351. *Fax:* 503/241-4370. *Tech. Support:* 503/241-1530. *Price:* $69.99. *Platform:* Macintosh, DOS. *Grade Level:* JH, HS. *Curriculum:* Sports.

A complete baseball library from 1871 to the 1991 World Series. Over 500 images of players, teams and ball parks, 2,600 pages of text, statistics of over 13,000 players, showing batting, pitching and fielding registers of all major league players and more.

Twain's World. Bureau for Electronic Publishing, 141 New Road, Parsippany, NJ 07054; 800/828-4766 (orders); 201/808-2700. *Fax:* 201/808-2676. *Tech. Support:* 201/808-2700, Ext. 22. *Price:* $39.95. *Platform:* MPC. *Grade Level:* JH, HS. *Curriculum:* Language Arts.

A multimedia program featuring Twain's work and personal life. Includes short

stories, essays, speeches, literary criticism and personal letters, period music, drawings and photographs.

UFO. Software Marketing Corp., 9830 South 51st Street, Building A131, Phoenix,
AZ 85044; 602/893-3377. *Fax:* 602/893-2042. *Tech. Support:* 602/893-8481. *Price:*
$59.95. *Platform:* Windows. *Grade Level:* JH, HS. *Curriculum:* Science.
   Contains over 1,200 sightings with photographs, full-motion video and audio.
Time span from 1000 B.C. to present. Search for specific sightings and UFO events
including contact and abduction reports.

Undersea Adventure. Knowledge Adventure, 4502 Dyer Street, La Crescenta, CA
91214; 800/542-4240 (orders); 818/248-0166 (bulletin board). *Fax:* 818/542-4205.
Tech. Support: 602/893-8481. *Price:* $59.95. *Platform:* Windows. *Grade Level:* Elem.,
JH, HS. *Curriculum:* Science.
   Seven entertaining and educational ways to explore a coral reef, the frigid waters
of the Arctic, or the deepest canyon on the planet — all within the hundred million
square miles of our planet's ocean.

U.S. History on CD-ROM. Bureau for Electronic Publishing, 141 New Road, Parsippany, NJ 07054; 800/828-4766 (orders); 201/808-2700. *Fax:* 201/808-2676. *Tech.
Support:* 201/808-2700, Ext. 22. *Price:* $395. *Platform:* Macintosh, DOS. *Grade Level:*
HS. *Curriculum:* Social Studies.
   Full text plus illustrations of 100 books covering political, social, economic and military perspective of pre–Revolutionary American history. Source materials comprise
public domain works published by U.S. Government.

U.S. History on CD-ROM. *Operating Systems:* DOS, MAC. *Subject:* United States
History. *Grade Level:* HS to Adult. *Hardware:* See distributor. *Software:* See distrib-
utor. *Distributor:* Updata.
   Contains the full texts of 107 history books, supplemented by more than 1,000 Super
VGA images, tables, maps and photos relating to historical events.

U.S. Presidents. Compton's New Media Inc., 2320 Camino Vida Roble, Carlsbad,
CA 92009; 800/862-2206; 800/216-6116 (catalog sales); 619/929-2500. *Fax:* 619/929-
2555. *Tech. Support:* 619/929-2626. *Price:* $39.95. *Platform:* DOS, Windows. *Grade
Level:* JH, HS. *Curriculum:* Social Studies.
   A collection of photographs, portraits, biographies and statistics of all presidents.
Statistical information is available on all the presidents including some of their wives.

U.S. Presidents. *Operating Systems:* DOS, MAC. *Subject:* U.S. Presidents. *Grade
Level:* General. *Hardware:* See distributor. *Software:* See distributor. *Distributor:*
Updata.
   Complete biographical and statistical information on the 42 men who have served
in the highest office of the land.

U.S. Presidents. Quanta Press, Inc., 1313 Fifth Street, Suite SE 223A, Minneapolis,
MN 55414; 612/379-3956. *Fax:* 612/623-4570. *Price:* $69.95. *Platform:* Macintosh,
DOS. *Grade Level:* JH, HS. *Curriculum:* Social Studies.
   Biographies, statistics and interesting information on the 41 men who have served
as president of the U.S. Includes data on first ladies.

The USA State Factbook. Operating Systems: DOS, MAC. *Subject:* United States Facts, Almanac. *Grade Level:* General. *Hardware:* See distributor. *Software:* See distributor. *Distributor:* Updata.

An almanac of the United States of America and its territories. Facts, figures and historical data on such subjects as geography, people, government, economies, communications, icons, traditions, even state fungi.

USA State Factbook. Quanta Press, Inc., 1313 Fifth Street, Suite SE 223A, Minneapolis, MN 55414; 612/379-3956. *Fax:* 612/623-4570. *Price:* $49.95. *Platform:* Macintosh, DOS, Windows. *Grade Level:* JH, HS. *Curriculum:* Social Studies.

An almanac of the United States of America.

USA Today: The '90s Volume 1. Operating System: MPC. *Subject:* News. *Grade Level:* General. *Hardware:* See distributor. *Software:* See distributor. *Distributor:* Updata.

Presents more than 40,000 of the most important and memorable stories from *USA Today's* news, money, sports and life sections. Also contains a world atlas, and the complete *Merriam-Webster Online Dictionary.*

USA Wars: Civil War. Compton's New Media Inc., 2320 Camino Vida Roble, Carlsbad, CA 92009; 800/862-2206; 800/216-6116 (catalog sales); 619/929-2500. *Fax:* 619/929-2555. *Tech. Support:* 619/929-2626. *Price:* $69.95. *Platform:* DOS, Windows. *Grade Level:* JH, HS. *Curriculum:* Social Studies.

Covering the years 1860–1865, this multimedia Civil War database includes biographies of prominent figures, chronologies, descriptions of campaigns and battles, statistics and photographs.

USA Wars: Civil War. Quanta Press, Inc., 1313 Fifth Street, Suite SE 223A, Minneapolis, MN 55414; 612/379-3956. *Fax:* 612/623-4570. *Price:* $69.95. *Platform:* Macintosh, DOS. *Grade Level:* HS. *Curriculum:* Social Studies.

Includes Civil War biographies, statistics, chronology, equipment, campaigns, battles, political figures, photographs, and music from the era played on period instruments.

USA Wars: Desert Storm. Operating Systems: DOS, MAC, Windows. *Subject:* Desert Storm. *Grade Level:* General. *Hardware:* See distributor. *Software:* See distributor. *Distributor:* Updata.

Contains text, images and sounds of the Persian Gulf War. Provides battle and weapons assessments, statistics and criticism.

USA Wars: Desert Storm with Coalition Command. Compton's NewsMedia Inc., 2320 Camino Vida Roble, Carlsbad, CA 92009; 800/862-2206; 800/216-6116 (catalog sales); 619/929-2500. *Fax:* 619/929-2555. *Tech. Support:* 619/929-2626. *Price:* $69.95. *Platform:* DOS, Windows. *Grade Level:* JH, HS.

Interact in a sophisticated strategy level simulation of the command and control activities that took place during military operations in the Middle East. In an actual battle, these rapid decisions are made by analyzing a host of changing variables.

USA Wars: Korea. Quanta Press, Inc., 1313 Fifth Street, Suite SE 223A, Minneapolis, MN 55414; 612/379-3956. *Price:* $69.95. *Platform:* Macintosh, DOS. *Grade Level:* HS. *Curriculum:* Social Studies.

True American heroes of the Korean War. Compilation of interviews and data collection of actual combat roles during Korean War.

USA Wars: Vietnam. *Operating Systems:* DOS, MAC. *Subject:* Vietnam War. *Grade Level:* General. *Hardware:* See distributor. *Software:* See distributor. *Distributor:* Updata.

Covers the United States' involvement in the Vietnam conflict. Includes special and general operations, order of battles, major unit histories, black-and-white and color battle images.

USA Wars: Vietnam. Quanta Press, Inc., 1313 Fifth Street, Suite SE 223A, Minneapolis, MN 55414; 612/379-3956. *Price:* $69.95. *Platform:* Macintosh, DOS. *Grade Level:* HS. *Curriculum:* Social Studies.

Covers the U.S. involvement in the Vietnam conflict. It contains 61,000 full-text records, order of battle, biographies, major unit histories, order of military rank, medals and awards.

USA Wars: World War II. Quanta Press, Inc., 1313 Fifth Street, Suite SE 223A, Minneapolis, MN 55414; 612/379-3956. *Fax:* 612/623-4570. *Price:* $79.95. *Platform:* Macintosh, DOS, Windows. *Grade Level:* HS. *Curriculum:* Social Studies.

United States' involvement in all theaters of operation from 1938 to 1945. Structured to be a photo archive of World War II with biographies, operations, battles and chronologies.

The View from Earth. Time Warner Interactive Group, 2210 West Olive Avenue, Burbank, CA 91506-2626; 800/593-6334; 818/955-9999. *Tech. Support:* 800/565-TWIG. *Price:* $79.99. *Platform:* Macintosh, MPC. *Grade Level:* HS. *Curriculum:* Science.

Based on the *Voyage Through the Universe* series from Time-Life Books, this interactive documentary details the July 11, 1991, eclipse. It features hundreds of illustrations and photographs, with maps, diagrams and explanatory text.

Webster's Interactive Encyclopedia. *Operating System:* Windows. *Subject:* General reference. *Grade Level:* General. *Hardware:* See distributor. *Software:* See distributor. *Distributor:* Updata.

Features 34,000 articles with more than 20,000 cross-references.

The Whale of a Tale. Texas Caviar Inc., 3933 Steck Avenue, Suite B115, Austin, TX 78759; 800/648-1719. *Fax:* 512/346-1393. *Tech. Support:* 512/346-7887. *Price:* $89.95; home, $49.95. *Platform:* Macintosh, Windows. *Grade Level:* Elementary, Middle. *Curriculum:* Language Arts.

A story of a whale that sets out to learn about electricity amusing enough in itself for youngsters. Story takes place during WWI and provides numerous historic details and music.

Whole Earth Catalog. *Operating System:* MAC. *Subject:* Reference. *Price:* $149.95. *Grade Level:* General. *Hardware:* See distributor. *Software:* See distributor. *Distributor:* Updata.

CD-ROM version of the best-selling *Whole Earth Catalog.* It includes more than 3,500 entries and covers a vast array of subjects — from building your own home to ultralight aircraft and city restoration. Includes a Hypercard feature which allows the user to move quickly from subject to subject. Contains more than 700 recordings from bird calls to jazz.

World Almanac and Book of Facts. Metatec Corporation, 7001 Metatec Boulevard, Dublin, OH 43017; 614/761-2000. *Fax:* 614/761-4258. *Tech. Support:* 614/766-3150. *Price:* $59.95. *Platform:* Macintosh. *Grade Level:* JH, HS. *Curriculum:* Reference and Interdisciplinary.

Over one million current facts. Contains full text of print version.

World Almanac and Book of Facts. *Operating Systems:* DOS, MAC. *Subject:* Almanac. *Grade Level:* General. *Hardware:* See distributor. *Software:* See distributor. *Distributor:* Updata.

One of the most comprehensive sources for reference information in the world. Arranged and indexed like the printed version, the almanac contains over one million up-to-date facts.

World Library Great Mystery Classics. World Library Inc., 2809 Main Street, Irvine, CA 92714; 800/443-0238; 714/756-9500. *Fax:* 714/756-9511. *Tech. Support:* 714/756-9550. *Price:* $49.95. *Platform:* Macintosh, DOS, Windows. *Grade Level:* HS. *Curriculum:* Language Arts.

Brings you the world of mystery, murder and suspense with 171 classic thrillers. Famous authors such as Conan Doyle, Stevenson and Verne are featured in this collection.

World Library Great Poetry Classics. World Library Inc., 2809 Main Street, Irvine, CA 92714; 800/443-0238; 714/756-9500. *Fax:* 714/756-9511. *Tech. Support:* 714/756-9550. *Price:* $49.95. *Platform:* Macintosh, DOS, Windows. *Grade Level:* HS. *Curriculum:* Language Arts.

Contains over 1,150 poems, sonnets and psalms from Blake to Keats.

World Library Greatest Books Collection. World Library Inc., 2809 Main Street, Irvine, CA 92714; 800/443-0238; 714/756-9500. *Fax:* 714/756-9511. *Tech. Support:* 714/756-9550. *Price:* $49.95. *Platform:* Macintosh, DOS, Windows. *Grade Level:* HS. *Curriculum:* Language Arts.

A collection of over 600 separate books, plays, poems and religious and historical documents.

World Library Shakespeare Study Guide. World Library Inc., 2809 Main Street, Irvine, CA 92714; 800/443-0238; 714/756-9500. *Fax:* 714/756-9511. *Tech. Support:* 714/756-9550. *Price:* $24.95. *Platform:* Macintosh, DOS, Windows. *Grade Level:* HS. *Curriculum:* Language Arts.

Shakespeare's complete works, including 37 plays, 5 poems, and 154 sonnets. Features *Barron's Book Notes* study guides for Shakespeare's most popular plays.

World Literary Heritage. *Operating Systems:* DOS, MAC, Windows. *Subject:* Literature. *Grade Level:* JH to Adult. *Hardware:* See distributor. *Software:* See distributor. *Distributor:* Updata.

Peruse the texts of more than 700 classic works of literature including poetry, fairy tales, novels and dramatic works, etc. Provides biographies accompanied by illustrations and narration.

World of Dinosaurs. *Operating System:* MAC. *Subjects:* Paleontology, dinosaurs. *Grade Level:* 1–5. *Hardware:* See distributor. *Software:* See distributor. *Distributor:* Updata.
Presents fascinating information on dinosaurs via animation, audio, video and print.

World Religions. *Operating System:* Windows. *Subject:* Comparative religions. *Grade Level:* HS to Adult. *Hardware:* See distributor. *Software:* See distributor. *Distributor:* Updata.
Explore Shamanism, Hinduism, Buddhism, Jainism, etc.

World View Media Clips. Aris Entertainment, 310 Washington Boulevard, Suite 100, Marina del Ray, CA 90292; 301/821-0234. *Fax:* 310/821-6463. *Price:* $39.95. *Platform:* Macintosh, DOS, Windows. *Grade Level:* HS. *Curriculum:* Arts and Music.
Photographs from NASA archives of the earth from above and of planets and outer space. Also contains originally composed piano and instrumental music.

World War II. *Operating System:* Windows. *Subject:* WWII. *Grade Level:* JH to Adult. *Hardware:* See distributor. *Software:* Windows 3.1. *Distributor:* Updata.
Includes video, audio, and graphic data covering over 2,100 events, including speeches by Churchill, Roosevelt, MacArthur and Hitler.

World War II Encyclopedia: The European Theater. *Operating System:* Windows. *Subject:* WWII. *Grade Level:* JH to Adult. *Hardware:* 386 CPU, 4MB RAM, 3MB disk space, audio card, mouse. *Software:* Windows 3.1, DOS 3.3, Extensions 2.2. *Distributor:* Updata.
Combines over 30 minutes of video, hundreds of photographs, and many documents and audio clips covering the war in Europe. Includes a notepad for recording research data without leaving the program.

World's Best Poetry. *Operating Systems:* DOS, Windows. *Subject:* Poetry. *Grade Level:* Not Given. *Hardware:* (DOS) 286 CPU, 525K RAM, (Windows) 386 CPU, 2MB RAM. *Software:* (DOS) DOS 3.3, (Windows) Windows 3.1, DOS 3.3. *Distributor:* Updata.
Full text of 3,000 poems by 1,200 poets, as well as 500 critical and biographical essays. Text search capability.

World's Greatest Speeches. *Operating System:* Windows. *Subject:* History. *Grade Level:* 5 to Adult. *Hardware:* 386 CPU, 4MB RAM, VGA, audio. *Software:* Windows 3.1, DOS 3.3. *Distributor:* Updata.
Includes one hour of audio, 30 minutes of video, pictures and biographies of the speakers, and the complete texts of speeches given by such historical figures as Christ, Hitler, Lincoln and John F. Kennedy.

Distributors/Producers

Distributors

Abt Books, Inc.
146 Mt. Auburn St.
Cambridge, MA 02138
(617) 661-1300
Sells and Rents databases.

Bureau of Electronic Publishing
141 New Road
Parsippany, NJ 07054
(800) 828-4766

CD One Stop
13 F. J. Clarke Circle
Bethel, CT 06801
(800) 826-0079
Wholesaler-CD's

CD-ROM, INC.
1667 Cole Blvd. Suite 400
Golden, CO 80401
(303) 231-9373

CDiscovery
Computerworks of Northport
260 Main St.
Northport, NY 11768
(800) 825-DISK

Compact Disc Products, Inc.
223 E. 85th St.
New York, NY 10028
(212) 737-8400
Fax: (212) 737-8289

EBSCO Publishing
P.O. Box 1943
Birmingham, AL 35201
(800) 826-3024, (205) 991-1182
Fax: (508) 887-3923
Producer and Distributor

FAXON Co.
15 Southwest Park
Westbrook, MA 02090
(800) FAXON, (617) 329-3350
Fax: (617) 326-5484

Gale Research, Inc.
P.O. Box 33477
Detroit, MI 48232-5477
(800) 877-GALE

New Media Source
Suite 2153
3830 Valley Centre Dr.
San Diego, CA 92130-9834
(800) 344-2621

University of Colorado
LASP-Campus Box 392
Boulder, CO 80309
(303) 492-7666

UPDATA
1736 Westwood Blvd.
Los Angeles, CA 90024
(800) 882-2844

Ztek Co.
P.O. Box 1968

Lexington, KY 40593
(800) 247-1603, (606) 252-7276

Producers

Abt Books, Inc.
146 Mt. Auburn St.
Cambridge, MA 02138
(617) 661-1300
Products: Real Estate database;
    National Portrait Gallery, The Per-
    manent Collection

Access Innovations, Inc.
P.O. Box 40130
4320 Mesa Grande S.E.
Albuquerque, NM 87196
(800) 421-8711, (505) 265-3591
Product: A-V ONLINE

Activism
2350 Bayshore Pkwy.
Mountain View, CA 94043
Product: Manhole (Mac)

AIRS, Inc.
Engineering Research Center
335 Paint Branch Drive
College Park, MD 20741
(301) 454-2022
Product: Bible Library

Alde Publishing
4830 W. 77th St.
P.O. Box 35326
Minneapolis, MN 55435
(612) 835-5240
Fax: (612) 835-3401

American Library Association
Information Technology Publishing
50 E. Huron St.
Chicago, IL 60611
(800) 545-2433, (312) 955-6780
Product: ALA CD-ROM

American Mathematical Society
P.O. Box 6248

Providence, RI 02940
(800) 556-7774, (401) 272-9500
Product: MathSciDisc

American Psychological Association
750 1st St. NE
Washington, DC 20002-4242
(800) 374-2721
Product: PsycLit

AMIGOS Bibliographic Council, Inc.
11300 N. Central Expressway
Suite 321
Dallas, TX 75243
(800) 843-8482, (214) 759-6130
Product: OCLC/AMIGOS Collection
    Analysis CD

Amtec Information Services
3700 Industry Ave.
Lakewood, CA 90714-6050
(213) 595-4756
Products: Exxon Corp. Basic Practices
    Manual; GE Aircraft Engines; Mack
    Elecronic Parts Disc

Apple Computer
20525 Mariani Ave.
Cupertino, CA 95014
(408) 973-6025
Product: Apple Science CD Volume I

Aries Systems Corp.
79 Boxford St.
North Andover, MA 01845-3219
(508) 689-9334
Products: CancerLit; Medline-Knowl-
    edge Finder

Auto-Graphics, Inc.
3201 Temple Ave.
Pomona, CA 91768
(800) 325-7961, (714) 595-7207
Products: GDCS Impact; Impact

Bell & Howell
5700 Lombardo Center

Suite 220
Seven Hills, OH 44131
(216) 642-9060
Products: Chrysler Parts Catalog; GM
  Parts Catalog; Honda Parts Catalog;
  Mercedes-Benz

Berkeley Macintosh User Group
2150 Kettredge 3b
Berkeley, CA 94709
(415) 549-2684
Product: CD-ROM (MAC)

BIOSIS
2100 Arch St.
Philadelphia, PA 19103-1399
(800) 523-4806, (215) 587-4800;
FAX (215) 587-2016
Product: Biological Abstracts

Blackwell North America, Inc.
6024 SW Jean Rd. Bldg. G
Lake Oswego, OR 97035
(503) 684-1140
Product: PC Order Plus

Bowker Electronic Publishing
245 W. 17th St.
New York, NY 10011
(800) 323-3288; (212) 337-6989;
FAX (212) 645-0475
Products: Books in Print Plus (IBM/
  Mac); Books in Print with Book
  Review Plus; Books Out of Print
  Plus; Ulrich's Plus; Variety's Video
  Directory Plus

Brodart Automation
500 Arch St.
Williamsport, PA 17705
(800) 233-8467, (717) 326-2461
Products: Access Pennsylvania; LePac;
  Government Documents Option;
  LePac: Interlibrary Loan; PC Rose
  System

Broderbund Software
17 Paul Dr.

San Rafael, CA 94903
(415) 479-1170
Product: Whole Earth Learning Disc
  (IBM/Mac)

Buchandler Vereinigung-GMBH
Gro Ber Hirschraben 17-21
Postfach 100442
6000 Frankfurt am Main 1, West Ger-
  many
Product: Verzeichnis Lieferbarer
  Bucher (German Books in Print sold
  by Chadwyck-Healy)

Buckmaster Publishing
Route 3 Box 56
Mineral, VA 23117
(800) 282-5628, (703) 894-5777
Product: Place-Name Index

C.A.B. International
Farnham House
Farnham Royal
Slough S12 3BN England
Product: CAB Abstracts

CD/Law Reports, Inc.
305 S. Hale, Suite 1
Wheaton, IL 60187
(312) 668-8895
Products: CD/Law: Illinois; Laserlaw
  Series

CD Plus
2901 Broadway, Suite 154
New York, NY 10025
(212) 932-1485
Products: CancerLit; Health; Medicine–CD Plus

CMC ReSearch
7150 S.W. Hampton, Suite 120
Portland, OR 97223
(503) 639-3395
Products: Cancer on Disc: 1988; Journal of Radiology; Pediatrics on Disc;
  Sherlock Holmes on Disc; Yearbook

Compact Cambridge
Cambridge Information Group
7200 Wisconsin Ave.
Bethesda, MD 20814
(800) 227-3052, (301) 961-6700
Products: Aquatic Sciences and Fish-
eries; Cancer Lit CD-ROM; Drug
Information Center; Life Sciences
Collection; Medline-Compact Cam-
bridge; PDQ CD-ROM (Physicians'
Data Query)

Compact Discoveries, Inc.
1050 S. Federal Highway
Delray Beach, FL 33444
(305) 243-1453
Products: Images Demo; Yellow Page
Demo

Computer Access Corp.
26 Brighton St., Suite 324
Belmont, MA 02178
(617) 484-2412
Products: CD-ROM: The New
Papyrus

Computer Aided Planning, Inc.
169-C Monroe N.W.
Grand Rapids, MI 49503
(616) 454-0000
Products: CAP (Computer Aided Programming)

Comstock, Inc.
30 Irving Pl.
New York, NY 10003
(212) 353-8686
Products: Desktop Photography (Mac)

Congressional Information Service,
Inc.
4520 East-West Highway, Suite 800
Bethesda, MD 20814-1550
(800) 638-8380, (301) 654-1550
Product: CIS Congressional Masterfile
1789-1969

Cornell University Distribution Center
7 Research Park
Ithaca, NY 14850
(607) 255-2901
Product: Black Fiction Up to 1920

Data Base Products, Inc.
12770 Coit Road, Suite 1111
Dallas, TX 75251-1314
(800) 345-3876, (214) 233-0595
Products: Form 41: Airline Carrier Fil-
ings; International: Airline Traffic;
Itineraries; O & D Plus Historical;
Onbard: Airline Traffic Data

DataTimes
1400 Quail Springs Pkwy., #450
Oklahoma City, OK 73134
(405) 451-6400
Products: Daily Oklahoman; Data
Times Libraries System; Washington
Post

Delorme Mapping Systems
P.O. Box 298
Freeport, ME 04032
(207) 865-4171
Product: Delorme's World Atlas

Deutsche Bibelgesellschaft
Balingerstrasse 31
7000 Stuttgart 80 East Germany
(49) 0711 71810
Product: Luther Bible

DIALOG Information Services
3460 Hillview Ave.
Palo Alto, CA 94304
(800) 3-DIALOG, (415) 858-3985
Products: DIALOG Ondisc; Canadian
Business and Current Affairs; ERIC;
Medline: Medline Clinical Collec-
tion: NTIS; Standard and Poor's
Corporations.

Digital Diagnostics, Inc.
601 University Ave.

Sacramento, CA 95825
(800) 826-5595, (916) 921-6629
Products: AIDS Supplement; Medline-BiblioMed; Medline-BiblioMed with AIDS Supplement; MetroScan

Digital Directory Assistance
561 River Rd.
Bethesda, MD 20816
(301) 657-8548
Product: Phone Disc

Disclosure
5161 River Rd.
Bethesda, MD 20816
(800) 843-7747, (301) 951-1300
Products: Compact Disclosure; Compact Disclosure–Europe; Disclosure Spectrum; Laser Disclosure: Commercial, Not for Profit, Wall Street

Discovery Systems
47001 Discovery Blvd.
Bublin, OH 43017
(614) 761-2000
Products: CD-ROM Sampler; Macintosh Showcase

Diversified Data Resources, Inc.
6609 Rosecraft P.I.
Falls Church, VA 22043-1828
(202) 237-0682
Product: The Sourcedisc

Donnelley Marketing Information Services
70 Seaview Ave.
P.O. Box 10250
Stamford, CT 06904
(800) 527-3647, (203) 353-7474
Product: Conquest: Consumer Information

Dun's Marketing Service
49 Old Bloomfield Rd.
Mountain Lakes, NJ 07046
(800) 526-0651, (201) 299-0181
Products: Business Information

EBSCO Electronic Information
P.O. Box 325
Topsfield, MA 01983
(800) 221-1826, (508) 887-6667
Products: Cataloger's Tool Kit; Comprehensive Medline; Core Medline; Reference Tool Kit; The Serials Directory

Education Systems Corp
6170 Cornerstone Court East, Suite 300
San Diego, CA 92121-3170
(619) 587-0087
Product: ESC Integrated Learning System

Educorp USA
531 Stephens Ave., Suite B
Solana Beach, CA 02075
(800) 843-9497, (619) 259-0255
Product: Public Domain Mac Programs (Macintosh)

Electromap, Inc.
P.O. Box 1153
Fayetteville, AR 72702-1153
Product: World Atlas

Electronic Text Corporation
2500 N. University Ave.
Provo, UT 84604
(801) 226-0616
Product: American Authors on CD-ROM

H.W. Wilson Co.
950 University Ave.
Bronx, NY 10452
(212) 588-8500
Products: Applied Science & Technology Index; Art Index; Biography Index; Biological and Agricultural Index; Book Review Digest; Business Periodicals Index; Cumulative Book Index; Education Index; Essay and General Literature Index; Film

Literature Index; General Science
Index; GPO Monthly Catalog Index
to Government Periodicals; Humani-
ties Index; Index to Legal Periodi-
cals; Library Literature; Modern
Language Assoc. Index; Reader's
Guide Abstracts; Reader's Guide to
Periodical Literature; Social Science
Index; WILSONDISC Demonstra-
tion Disc

Virginia Polytechnic Institute
Blacksburg, VA 24061
(703) 231-6000
Product: Virginia Disk

Voyager Co.
1351 Pacific Coast Hwy.
Santa Monica, CA 90401
(213) 451-1383
Product: CD Companion–Beethoven
   Symphony No. 9

Walters Lexicon Co.
Sodermalmstrong 8,
17800 Stockholm, Sweden
Product: Termdox

Yellow Pages

CD-ROM Publishers/
Distributors

Artfact, Inc.
1130 Ten Rod Road
Suite E104
North Kingstown, RI 02852
(401) 295-2656 Fax (401) 295-2629

Baker & Taylor
2709 Water Ridge Parkway
Charlotte, NC 28217
(800) 775-1800

BiblioFile
The Library Corporation Research Park

Inwood, WV 25428-9733
(800) 325-7759, (404) 591-0089
Fax (404) 591-0334

Chadwyck-Healey, Inc.
1101 King Street
Suite 380
Alexandria, VA 22314-2944
(800) 752-0515, (703) 683-4890
Fax (703) 683-7589

Dialog Information Services
3460 Hillview Ave.
Palo Alto, CA 94304
(800) 334-2564, (415) 858-3785
Fax (415) 858-7069

Information Access Company
Info Trac Sales & Customer Svc.
362 Lakeside Dr.
Foster City, CA 94404
(800) 227-8431, (415) 378-5000
Fax (415) 378-5369

Information Access Company
   EUROPE
Watergate House
13-15 York Buildings
London WC2N 6JU
In Europe: +44-(0)71 930 3933
Fax: +44-(0)71 930 9190

Library of Congress
CDS, Customer Services
Section/Dept., ZD
Washington, DC 20541
(800) 255-3666, (202) 707-6100
Fax (202) 707-1334

Modern Talking Pictures
5000 Park Street North
St. Petersburg, FL 33709
(800) 237-4599

Predicasts
362 Lakeside Dr.
Foster City, CA 94404

(800) 321-6388
Fax (415) 358-4759

Softec Plus
4021 E. Grant Rd., #201
Tuscon, AZ 85712
(800) 779-1991
Fax (602) 325-5402

UMI (University Microfilms, Inc.)
300 North Zeeb Road
Ann Arbor, MI 48106-1346
(800) 521-0600, (313) 761-4700
Fax (800) UMI-0019

UPDATA Publications, Inc.
1736 Westwood Blvd.
Los Angeles, CA 90024
(800) 882-2844, (310) 474-5900
Fax (310) 474-4095

Westland Education Resources
Suite 300, 2899 Agoura Rd.
Westlake Village, CA 91361
(800) 543-1707
Fax (805) 495-7123

WLN
P.O. Box 3888
Lacey, WA 98503-088
(800) 342-5956, (206) 923-4000
Fax (206) 923-4009

CD-ROM Storage & Display

Alps, Inc.
P.O. Box 1409
Cary, NC 27512-1409
(800) 344-8363, (919) 365-3141
Fax (919) 365-3699

Can-Am Merchandising
900 Hertel Avenue
Buffalo, NY 14216
70 Shields Court
Markham, Ont. Canada L3R 9T5
(800) 387-9790, (905) 475-6622
Fax (905) 475-1154

Demco, Inc.
4810 Forest Run Rd.
P.O. Box 7488
Madison, WI 53707
(800) 356-1200, (608) 241-1201
Fax (800) 245-1329

J.B. Engineering
1714 California Ave.
Monrovia, CA 91016
(800) 523-3432, (818) 303-2626
Fax (818) 358-1546

Mr. Video
6827 Valjean Avenue
Van Nuys, CA 91406
(800) 432-4336, (818) 789-7238
Fax (818) 785-1238

Russ Bassett
8189 Byron Road
Whittier, CA 90606
(800) 350-2445
Fax (310) 698-8972

CD-ROM Wholesalers

Baker & Taylor
2709 Water Ridge Parkway
Charlotte, NC 28217
(800) 775-1800

Midwest Tape Exchange
1750 West Laskey Rd.
Toledo, OH 43613
(800) 875-2785, (419) 417-0836
Fax (419) 417-1029

Advertising Industry

National Register Publishing
A Reed Reference Publishing Co.
121 Chanlon Road
New Providence, NJ 07974
(800) 521-8110
Fax (908) 665-6688

Automotive Repair

Mitchell International
9889 Willow Creek Rd.
P.O. Box 26260
San Diego, CA 92196
(800) 238-9111, (619) 578-6550
Fax (619) 566-3345

Bibliographic Information

Baker & Taylor
2709 Water Ridge Parkway
Charlotte, NC 28217
(800) 775-1800

Bibliographic Management

BiblioFile
The Library Corporation Research
   Park
Inwood, WV 25428-9733
(800) 325-7759, (404) 591-0089
Fax (404) 591-0334

Books in Print

R.R. Bowker
A Reed Reference Publishing Co.
121 Chanlon Road
New Providence, NJ 07974
(800) 323-3288
Fax (908) 665-3528

Books in Print — International

R.R. Bow Baker
A Reed Reference Publishing Co.
121 Chanlon Road
New Providence, NJ 07974
(800) 323-3288
Fax (908) 665-3528

Books in Print — Spanish Language

R.R. Bowker
A Reed Reference Publishing Co.
121 Chanlon Road

New Providence, NJ 07974
(800) 323-3288
Fax (908) 665-3528

Calendars-Storytelling

Stotter Press
Storytelling Calendar
P.O. Box 726
Stinson Beach, CA 94970
(415) 435-3568
Fax (415) 435-9923

Careers

Federal Jobs Digest
325 Pennsylvania Ave. SE
Washington, DC 20003
(800) 824-5000, (914) 762-5111

Children's Reference Materials

R.R. Bowker
A Reed Reference Publishing Co.
121 Chanlon Road
New Providence, NJ 07974
(800) 323-3288
Fax (908) 665-3528

Code of Federal Regulations

Counterpoint Publishing
84 Sherman Street
P.O. Box 928
Cambridge, MA 02140
(800) 998-4515
Fax (617) 547-9064

College Catalogs

Career Guidance Foundation
8090 Engineer Rd.
San Diego, CA 92111
(800) 854-2670, (619) 560-8051
Fax (619) 278-8960

Corporate Information

Disclosure Incorporated
5161 River Road

Bethesda, MD 20816
(800) 945-3647, (301) 961-2789
Fax (301) 718-2343

Dun & Bradstreet Information
  Services
3 Sylvan Way
Parsippany, NJ 07054
(800) 526-0651, Fax (201) 605-6911

Extel Financial, Inc.
40 Richards Ave.
Norwalk, CT 06854
(203) 857-7400, (203) 857-7444

Moody's Investors Service
99 Church St.
New York, NY 10007
(800) 955-8080, (212) 553-4700

National Register Publishing
A Reed Reference Publishing Co.
121 Chanlon Road
New Providence, NJ 07974
(800) 521-8110
Fax (908) 665-6688

Economics

American Economic Association
(Journal of Economic Literature)
P.O. Box 7320
Pittsburgh, PA 15213-0320
(412) 268-3869
Fax (412) 268-6810

Educational

Bureau of Electronic Publishing
141 New Road
Parsippany, NJ 07054
(800) 828-4766, (201) 808-2700

Follett Software Company
809 N. Front Street
McHenry, IL 60050-5589
(800) 323-3397, (815) 344-8700
Fax (815) 344-8774

Encyclopedias & Dictionaries

Random House Reference
Random House, Inc.
201 East 50th Street
New York, NY 10022
(800) 733-3000, (212) 940-7394

Environment

ERM Computer Services, Inc.
912 Springdale Drive
Exton, PA 19341
(800) 365-2146
Fax (215) 594-4481, (215) 594-4400

Ethnic/Minority Press

SoftLine Information, Inc.
(Ethnic NewsWatch)
65 Broad Street
Stamford, CT 06901
(800) 524-7922, (203) 975-8292
Fax (203) 975-8347

Genealogy

GenSys Automated Resource Files
175 North Freedom Blvd.
Provo, UT 84601
(801) 375-6591
Fax (801) 375-6975

Government Publications

BiblioFile
The Library Corporation Research
  Park
Inwood, WV 25428-9733
(800) 325-7759, (404) 591-0089
Fax (404) 591-0334

Government Publications — U.S.

MARCIVE, Inc.
P.O. Box 47508
San Antonio, TX 78265
(800) 531-7678, (210) 646-6161
Fax (210) 646-0167

Staff Directories, Ltd.
LOCATOR CD-ROM
P.O. Box 62
Mount Vernon, VA 22121
(703) 739-0990
Fax (703) 739-0234

Humanities

InteLex Corporation
P.O. Box 1827
Clayton, GA 30525-1827
(706) 782-7844
Fax (706) 782-4489

Insurance Industry

A.M. Best
Ambest Road
Oldwick, NJ 08858
(908) 439-2200
Fax (908) 439-3296

Library Management

BiblioFile
The Library Corporation Research
    Park
Inwood, WV 25428-9733
(800) 324-7759, (404) 591-0089
Fax (404) 591-0334

Brodart Automation
500 Arch Street
Williamsport, PA 17705
(800) 233-8467, (800) 666-9162
(717) 326-2461
Fax (717) 327-9237

Literary Reference

Salem Press
580 Sylvan Ave.
Englewood Cliffs, NJ 07632
(800) 221-1592, (201) 871-3700
Fax (201) 871-8668

Maps

Delorme Mapping Co.
P.O. Box 298
Lower Main St.
Freeport, ME 04032
(800) 452-5931, (207) 865-1234
Fax (207) 865-9291

Medical Information

Medical Economics Data
5 Paragon Drive
Montvale, NJ 07645
(800) 526-4570, (201) 358-7383
(800) 223-0581
Fax (201) 573-8999

Networked Databases

BiblioFile
The Library Corporation Research
    Park
Inwood, WV 25428-9733
(800) 325-7759, (404) 591-0089
Fax (404) 591-0334

CD PLUS Technologies
333 7th Avenue
New York, NY 10001
(800) 950-2035, (212) 563-3006
Fax (212) 563-3784

SilverPlatter Information
100 River Ridge Drive
Norwood, MA 02062
(800) 343-0064, (617) 769-2599
Fax (908) 769-8763

Periodicals

R.R. Bowker
A Reed Reference Publishing Co.
121 Chanlon Road
New Providence, NJ 07974
(800) 323-3288
Fax (908) 665-3528

Poetry

Columbia University Press
136 South Broadway
Irvington, NY 10533
(800) 944-8648, (914) 591-9111
Fax (800) 944-1844

Roth Publishing
185 Great Neck Road
Great Neck, NY 11021
(800) 899-roth, (516) 466-3676
Fax (516) 829-7746

Reference

SilverPlatter Information
100 River Ridge Drive
Norwood, MA 02062
(800) 343-0064, (617) 769-2599
Fax (908) 769-8763

Science

R.R. Bowker
A Reed Reference Publishing Co.
121 Chanlon Road
New Providence, NJ 07974
(800) 323-3288
Fax (908) 665-3528

Salem Press
580 Sylvan Ave.
Englewood Cliffs, NJ 07632
(800) 221-1592, (201) 871-3700
Fax (201) 871-8668

Statistics

Slater Hall Information Products
1301 Pennsylvania Ave. NW, Suite 507
Washington, DC 20004
(202) 393-2666
Fax (202) 638-2248

Telephone Directories

Metromall Corporation
360 E. 22nd St.
Lombard, IL 60148
(800) 793-2536
Fax (708) 620-3014

USMARC

Follett Software Company
809 N. Front Street
McHenry, IL 60050-5589
(800) 323-3397, (815) 344-8700
Fax (815) 344-8774

Glossary

AACR2R ANGLO-AMERICAN CATALOGUING RULES, second edition, 1988 revision.

abstract The summary of a document.

access Information retrieval from memory or mass storage.

access point A title for retrieving a catalog record.

access time The number of milliseconds between issuing a search command and obtaining the information.

acoustic modem A modem that uses the handset of an ordinary telephone to transmit and receive data.

ADC Analog to Digital Conversion. Converts analog data or signals to digital format for a computer to use.

address A digital code which indicates the location of an item on a CD-ROM or in memory.

AI Artificial Intelligence. Software which mimics human responses and problem solving abilities.

algorithm 1) A formula used in programming a computer. 2) Any set of instructions. 3) A step-by-step procedure from arriving at a solution to a problem.

aliasing Distortion of digital data that occurs when the sample rate is too low.

analog An infinitely variable signal such as time or temperature.

analog monitor A monitor that displays an unlimited range of brightness for each color.

analog video A video signal that represents an infinite number of smooth gradations between given video levels.

ANSI American National Standards Institute.

anti-aliasing Combating jagged edges in images by averaging the pixels along the edges.

application A word used with program and software.

application program A program that performs work not related to the computer itself.

application software Programs designed to perform a user specific task such as word processing.

architecture The composition of a system described to convey its components' inter-relationships and purposes.

archive A filing system for information to be kept indefinitely.

ARCnet A local area network developed in 1977 by Datapoint Corporation.

ASCII   American Standard Code for Information Interchange. A seven bit code to represent numbers, letters, and control characters.

aspect ratio   The relationship of width and height.

audio track   The section of a CD-ROM that contains the sound signal.

audiovisual   Nonprint materials such as films, cassettes, and slides.

authoring system   Software designed to help a nonprogrammer develop a multimedia or hypertext application.

AUTOEXEC.BAT   A file executed when the computer is booted to establish the computer's working environment.

average latency   The average amount of time for a CD-ROM drive to find a particular data sector.

back up   To make a copy of a program or file in case the original is damaged.

backbone network   A network to which smaller networks are attached.

bandwidth   The range of signal frequencies that audio or video equipment can accept.

barcode   Using bars of different widths and lengths to represent numeric data.

baseband   Digital information transmitted across the entire width of a cable.

baud   The number of bits per second transmitted during communications. Usually 300, 1200, 2400, or 9800 baud.

beta testing   The second level of testing for new software that occurs at external sites.

bibliographic citation   A reference to an original source of information.

binary   Consisting of two parts.

bios   Basic Input/Output system. Software built into an IBM-compatible's ROM that allows the computer to interact with I/O devices such as monitors and printers.

bit   The smallest unit of a computer, represented by a 1 or 0.

bit specifications   The number of colors or levels of gray that can be displayed on a computer monitor at once.

bitmap   The arrangement of pixels on a computer monitor to display an image.

bitmapped graphics   Pictures created with bitmap software.

board   A printed circuit.

Boolean logic   A logical system of searching by combining groups of words with AND, OR, or NOT.

Boolean search   A search strategy that uses Boolean logic.

boot   To start a computer.

bps   bits per second. Measures the speed of data transmission.

branching   Moving nonsequentially from one part of a program to another.

bridge   A device that links two LANs.

broadcast quality   A U.S. standard of 525 lines of video picture information.

brouter   A combination of bridge and router for linking LANs.

browse   To search online through an index or list of topics.

buffer   A small portion of computer memory allocated to store data temporarily.

built-in   Drives mounted internally into a computer.

bundling   Selling computer hardware with preselected peripherals and software.

burst transmission   Transmitting data intermittently in groups.

bus   A pathway between hardware devices.

button   A visible spot on a computer screen that activates a link to another location.

byte The amount of space needed to store in memory one character. A single byte normally consists of eight bits.

cables Various lines used to transmit data.

cache A place to temporarily store data to avoid reading it from a slower device.

caching Temporarily storing data in anticipation of the user's next search request.

caddy The plastic container that holds and protects a CD when it is inserted into a CD-ROM player.

CAI Computer Aided Instruction.

carrier An electric wave or alternating current.

catalog A list of the contents of a disk.

CAV Constant Angular Velocity. A method of recording and reading data on a disk while the disk spins at a constant speed.

CBT Computer Based Training.

CD Compact Disc. A 12 cm plastic optical disc used to store large amounts of data.

CD-DA Compact Disc–Digital Audio. The music disc first developed by Sony and Philips in 1980.

CD-I Compact Disc Interactive. A Philips proprietary CD format containing pre-recorded digital video, audio, and optical text data.

CD-R CD-Recordable.

CD-ROM Compact Disc–Read Only Memory. Information on the disc cannot be erased or altered.

CD-ROM XA CD-ROM Extended Architecture. The standard for interleaving or alternating audio graphics or text data.

CDTV A Commodore self-contained multimedia system.

CGA Color Graphics Adapter. Displays four colors on IBM-compatibles. Software written for CGA can usually be used with EGA and VGA monitors also.

CGM Computer Graphics Metafile. A standard image interchanging format.

channel A path along which data flows.

character A number, letter, or other symbol which is uniquely expressed in computer code.

character string Any group of characters used as a single unit by a computer system.

chip Chips are devices made of highly refined silicon to be used for memory or computer controls.

classification system Arranging information according to subject.

client A node on a network that requests service from another node.

clip art Graphic images that can be freely reproduced.

clock A circuit that generates evenly spaced pulses.

clone A computer that is an imitation of another computer or software that is an imitation of another software.

CLV Constant Linear Velocity. A method of recording and reading data on a disk.

CMYK Cyan, magenta, yellow, and black. The colors used in four-color printing.

coaxial cable A well-shielded, insulated cable used for networks with a central conductor.

color graphics A bit-mapped graphics display for IBM-compatible computers. Displays four colors simultaneously with a resolution of 200 pixels horizontally and 320 pixels vertically and displays one color with a resolution of 640 pixels horizontally and 200 vertically.

command   A computer instruction to perform a task.

command search   Software that accepts direct commands from a computer to conduct data searches.

communications software   Software installed to allow communication and data transmission between computers.

compatible   An adjective that describes hardware and software that can be used with a specific type of computer.

compression   Reducing the size of a file by removing unused space.

computer system   A complete computer installation including peripherals.

concentrator   The central hub of a star topology LAN.

CONFIG.SYS   A file executed when a computer is started.

configure   To set up a computer or program to be used in a specific way.

connectivity   The ability to transmit data from one device to another.

continuous tone   An image that uses all of the gray or color values.

contrast   The range between dark and light tones.

controlled vocabulary   Specific terms used in the search of a database.

controller   Any hardware or software elements that handles data communications between a computer and a peripheral device.

conventional memory   IBM-compatible RAM memory for 0 to 1024K.

conversion   The process of transferring information recorded in one format to another format.

coprocessor   A separate circuit inside a computer that handles extra work for the CPU while the CPU is completing other tasks.

CPU   Central Processing Unit. The "brains" of a computer.

crash   When a hardware or software error causes the computer to become inoperable.

CRT   Cathode Ray Tube. The computer monitor.

cursor   A small, flashing symbol that indicates the current location on a computer screen at which new data may be entered.

DAC   Digital to Analog Conversion.

daisychain   A way of attaching up to seven peripheral devices to a single SCSI port.

daisywheel printer   Printer which uses a rotating plastic wheel as a type element.

data   Information.

data buffer   For CD-ROM, where portions of data are temporarily stored while the drive accessed more data.

Data Discman   Hand-held CD-ROM player made by Sony.

data entry   Adding information to a database or other storage facility.

data export   Sending out images or files from one program or computer to another.

data import   Bringing in files from one program or computer to another.

data preparation   Readying a database for CD-ROM manufacture.

database   A collection of similar types of information stored as fields and records.

dataware   A collection of data only compatible with specific search software.

debug   The process of finding and correcting errors in a program.

decompression   Expansion of compressed data.

dedicated line   A telephone line reserved for a specific use.

dedicated server   A large computer on a network reserved exclusively as the server.

default   The assumption that a computer or program makes unless it is given specific instructions to the contrary.

delivery system   Hardware and software required to play a multimedia presentation.

descriptor   Specific word or phrase used to identify a specific type or subject of a data record.

device driver   Software that controls the CD-ROM drive.

digital   A discretely variable signal or characteristic such as a pulse or digitized image as opposed to an infinitely variable analog signal.

digital video   A video signal represented in binary format.

digitize   To convert data into a form the computer can recognize and use.

directory   An area where the names and locations of files are stored.

disk caching   Placing frequently used data in RAM for faster access.

disk capacity   The storage capacity of a floppy disk or a hard disk, measured in kilobytes or megabytes.

disk drive   Hardware required to access a disk.

disk server   A large computer that functions as a server on a network.

display   Information on a computer screen. A term for a computer monitor or terminal.

DMA   Direct Memory Access. A circuit for data transmission that does not use the main processor.

document   A term for any file created with a computer application.

documentation   The guides and manuals that come with a computer hardware or software package.

DOS   Disk Operating System. The set of instructions IBM-compatible computers need to function and interact with peripherals and software.

Dot-Matrix Printer   A printer that creates characters by striking an inked ribbon with needle-like pins.

double speed drive   A CD-ROM drive that transfers text and graphics at 300KB/sec and audio at 150KB/sec.

download   To transfer data from one computer to another.

dump   To transfer data from one place to another with regard for its significance.

DVI   Digital Video Interactive. Intel's process for compressing full motion video and audio onto CD-ROM or hard disk so that it can be played back on IBM multimedia systems.

EGA   Enhanced Graphics Adapter. Displays 16 high resolution colors on IBM compatibles.

electronic mail (e-mail)   Messages sent between computers connected by a network or by telephone lines.

emulation   Imitation of one device by another.

encode   To convert data into machine-readable format.

end-user   The person who will actually use requested information.

Enter/Return   A key that begins a command by sending it to the CPU.

error correction   The addition of an error-correction code to each block of data during CD-ROM premastering to ensure error detection and correction.

error detection   Coding that will find errors but not correct them.

Ethernet   A baseband LAN developed by XEROX.

expanded memory   The portion of RAM that must be added or emulated to run some programs for IBM-compatibles.

expert system   A program that uses stored information to perform a difficult task usually performed by a human expert.

extended memory   Any memory beyond the first megabyte of RAM in IBM-compatibles.

extensions   Programs added to an operating system to add capabilities.

external drive   see   **disk drive**.

fax   Common name for facsimile transmissions. Uses telephone lines to transmit an image of a document.

fiber optic cable   Lines that use light rather than electricity to transmit signals.

field   A distinct part of the records in a database that contain similar data.

file   A single, logical set of data.

file server   A LAN node that serves as the storage and distribution center for other LAN nodes.

file sharing   More than one LAN node accessing a file.

filter   A computer program to eliminate database irregularities before CD-ROM mastering occurs.

floppy disk   A removable, portable magnetic storage medium.

FMV   Full Motion Video. Video reproduction at 30 frames-per-second.

font   The complete set of characters for a typeface.

format   Characteristics of a document including size, margins, font, platform, etc.

fractals   Graphics software that converts the outline of an object into mathematical formulas.

frame   One picture in video or film.

frame grabber   Computer software or hardware designed to capture and save a single frame.

frame rate   Frame display speed.

free-text   To search every word of a database for a desired text.

frequency   The oscillation rate of a signal.

full text   A document in a database that contains the entire original.

function key   A key on a keyboard that activates a specific command.

gain   To increase an audio signal.

gateway   A translation device to link unlike computers.

genlock   Locking two video signals together so they begin together and run at the same rate.

gigabyte   Approximately a thousand megabytes.

gradient   A smooth blend from one color to another.

Graphical User Interface (GUI)   A visual interface for computers such as Windows.

graphics   Portrayed information such as pictorial representations, charts, and graphs.

Green Book   The common name for the CD-I Standards.

hard disk   A computer's permanent magnetic storage medium.

hardcopy   Paper or print version of machine readable data.

hardware   The physical components of a computer system.

HDTV   High Definition Television. A standard for a higher resolution, wider ranged television picture.

HFS   Hierarchical File Structure. The design of the operating system used by Macintosh computers.

high resolution   More pixels per square inch than standard resolution.

High Sierra   A standardized format for placing files on a CD-ROM.

hit   An item found in a search.

HSB   Hue, Saturation, Brightness. Allows the definition of colors by percentages.

hub   The central device in a star topology LAN.

Hypercard   An authoring system which is used to create interactive applications.

hypermedia   Linking text, graphics, audio, etc. together nonsequentially.

hypertext   Text linked nonsequentially, with instant access to parts by menus.

icon   A picture that represents a function in a graphical interface.

ID switches   One or more switches that assign an ID number to a CD drive.

image   A picture.

image resolution   The measurement in dots per inch of a digitized picture's resolution.

Imagination Machine   Desktop CD-I player by Phillips.

index searching   see **descriptor**.

information retrieval   Extracting data from a database.

initialize   To start for the first time.

input   To enter data into a computer or the data entered.

interactive   Software that allows users to use a computer according to their own needs. It allows choices and branching at many points.

Interactive Videodisc   CAI technology that uses a computer to provide access to up to two hours of video information on videodisc.

interface   A hardware link between two systems or a link between a user and a system.

interlace   Using two vertical scans to display video images.

interleave   To mix different data streams so they can be played simultaneously.

internal drive   Disk drive.

interrupt   A command that tells the computer to stop its present operation, save its location, and do something else.

I/O   Input/Output.

IPX   Internet Packet Exchange. Novell's Netware communications protocol to route messages between nodes.

ISDN   Integrated Services Digital Network. A telephone service for transmitting data.

ISO   International Standards Organization. Establishes and manages standards for digitizing video and audio.

ISO 8879   Standard Graphics Markup Language (SGML). The standard for exchange of electronic text.

ISO 9660   Creates a standard format for files on a CD-ROM.

jewel box   Plastic box in which most CDs are packaged.

joystick   An input device used primarily for games that is similar to the throttle stick in an airplane.

jukebox   One single CD-ROM drive mechanism that can swap between four to six disks.

KB/sec   Kilobytes per second.

keyword   Any searchable word in a database.

kilobyte   1024 bytes.

kilohertz   1000 cycles per second.

KWIC   Keyword in Context. Retrieval of a keyword along with part of the record in which it appears in a database.

LAN Local Area Network. A group of computers connected together with cabling and software.

lands The reflective areas between nonreflective pits on a CD-ROM.

language Refers to a special set of instructions by which the computer is programmed to operate or by which data may be manipulated.

laser Light Amplification by Stimulated Emission of Radiation. Optical media is created and read by a laser beam.

laser printer Uses a laser beam to generate an image and then transfers the image electronically to paper.

laserdisc see **videodisc.**

latency The delay on a CD-ROM while the disk rotates to the position to access data.

LCD Liquid Crystal Display. A display usually found on portable and laptop computers.

leased line A telephone line supplied by the phone company to connect only two points.

LED A type of semiconductor frequently used to signal on/off conditions in toggle keys.

linear A sequence read from beginning to end.

link A connection of two nodes in a hypertext database.

load To transfer data from a disk into the computer's RAM.

local area network see **LAN.**

Local Talk A network standard used on Macintosh computers.

logoff To end a computing session.

logon To connect to a computing group. Usually requires a user name and password.

machine-readable Data that a computer can read.

MARC Machine-Readable Catalog.

master An original recording of a finished program.

mastering Producing an original recording mold on a glass disk to be used to stamp out multiple optical disks.

MCI Media Control Interface. Microsoft specification for multimedia device control.

megabyte Approximately one million bytes.

megahertz The number of cycles per second on a particular frequency that equals one million cycles per second.

memory The amount of RAM in any given computer.

menu A list of available functions provided by the software.

menu bar The graphically highlighted bar that indicates the choice to be used in a menu program.

menu-driven search A method of searching for information by choosing menu functions.

microprocessor Hardware that performs the logic functions of digital computers.

MIDI Musical Instrument Digital Interface. The data bus standard for exchanging information between musical instruments and computers.

MMPC MultiMedia Portable Computer.

modeling Software that replicates real-life situations.

modem A device that converts digital signals to analog and vice-versa to send data over a telephone line.

monitor Video display unit for a computer.

motion video A sequence of images displayed fast enough to give the impression of motion.

mouse A hand-operated device used to move a cursor on the terminal and perform functions by clicking buttons.

MPC Multimedia Personal Computer. Minimum requirements are a 386 machine with 2MB of RAM, a hard drive, Windows 3.1, a VGA monitor, a CD-ROM drive, and a sound card.

MSCDEX Microsoft CD-ROM Extensions. Additions to DOS that helps a hard drive operate a CD-ROM drive and process large files.

MTBF Mean Time Between Failures. A method used to measure a hardware's reliability.

multidrive player A CD-ROM player with four drive mechanisms.

multimedia The ability to run various kinds of data in one application (text, graphics, motion, sound).

multiplayer A disk playing system consisting of multiple CD-ROM player units controlled by one computer.

multisession A CD-ROM XA drive that reads Kodak Photo CDs that contain more than one photo session.

Multi-User System A computer system that enables more than one user to access programs and data at the same time.

navigate To move nonsequentially between nodes in a hypermedia database.

near letter quality Printer output that resembles the print of a cloth-ribbon typewriter.

NETBIOS Network Basic Input/Output System. IBM software to interface LANs, DOS, and applications.

NetWare Novell Inc. network operating system.

network Computers connected by cable that have the ability to share programs, peripherals, and files.

networking Connection of more than one computer or peripheral together.

NIC Network Interface Card.

NISO National Information Standards Organization. Establishes U.S. standards for libraries, information sciences, and publishing.

node A workstation on a LAN. An entry point in a hypermedia database.

NOS Network Operation System. A set of computer instructions for managing LAN resources and activities.

NTSC National Television Standard Committee. Sets the standard for U.S. television transmission.

OCR Optical Character Recognition. Software that converts a scanned bitmap image of text into digital text the computer understands.

online Any computer activity while it is running, accessing an electronic database, or using a modem.

online searching Using a computer to access a database on a different computer.

operating system System software to control a computer's internal functions.

optical Computer systems that use laser technology for data.

optical server   A server that provides users to access the same CD-ROM drives at the same time.

Orange Book   The standards for CD-ROM WORM.

output   The information that the computer generates as a result of its calculations.

overlay   Adding text or graphics onto existing motion video.

packet   Information in binary format transmitted to and from LAN nodes.

parallel port   A port where peripheral devices can be connected to a computer so that data can be passed in parallel rows.

password   A confidential and unique string that restricts users from unauthorized access.

PC   Personal Computer.

PCX   A graphics file format.

peripheral   Hardware devices connected to and controlled by a computer.

Photo CD   The CD-ROM standard for storing and viewing digitized color images from photographs. Developed by Philips and Kodak.

PIC   A graphics file format.

PICT   A graphics file format.

pits   The microscopic, nonreflective indentations on a CD.

pixel   A condensed form of "picture element." It is a single point on a display.

polycarbonate   Plastic used to make CDs.

port   A computer socket for connecting peripherals with a cable.

power surge   A large increase in line voltage caused by a power outage.

premastering   The preparation of mastering information for pressing onto an optical disc.

printer   A device used to make a copy of file on paper.

printout   The paper record of a computer file.

program   A set of instructions to perform a task. Also, software or application.

prompt   An indication that the computer is waiting for information.

proprietary file format   A file format developed by a firm to be used for the storage of data created by its products. The format is usually unreadable by other application programs.

protocol   Rules that govern the transmission of data between hardware.

proximity search   An online search that tells the physical closeness of keywords. Indicated by "next to," "within," etc.

public domain   Material that is not copyrighted.

QuickTime   Apple Macintosh software that consolidates video, sound and animation.

RAM   Random Access Memory. Temporary data stored in a computer with rapid and nonsequential access. Erased when the computer is off.

raster   A pattern of scanning an image from left to right and top to bottom.

raster graphics   Bitmapped graphics.

read   Retrieve data from computer storage.

real-time   Processing data immediately without storage or offline processing.

reboot   To restart a computer.

recall   Number of records retrieved into a database.

record   A collection of information related to one subject.

Red Book   Standard for creating CD-Audio discs.

relevance   The ratio of the number of relevant records retrieved during a search to the total number of records in the database.

repeater   A device to boost signal transmission.

replication   The production of multiple copies of a CD-ROM master disk.

reset button   A button that enables you to reboot if the system cannot be restarted using the reset keys.

reset keys   A key combination used to reboot a computer system (Ctrl-Alt-Del on DOS systems).

resolution   The number of pixels in an area of a screen.

retrieval program   Search software.

RGB   Red, Green, Blue. A type of computer monitor with separately controlled color output.

ring   A network topology where nodes are connected in a closed loop.

Rock Ridge Group   Promoters of UNIX-based 9660 standards.

ROM   Read Only Memory. Internal memory used by the computer for its own purposes.

root directory   The main directory of a disk containing files and subdirectories.

router   A device that selects the best path for sending data between LANs.

RS 232C   Standard serial port for connecting peripheral devices.

runtime system   Delivery system.

sampling   Measuring the values of an analog signal at intervals, then encoding the signals to create a corresponding digital signal.

scanner   Hardware device that converts information on paper to bitmapped computer graphics.

SCSI   Small Computer System Interface. An eight-bit parallel bus interface for connecting devices to a computer.

search engine   Search software.

SECAM   Sequential Coleur Avec Mémoire. The French standard for color television transmission.

sector   The smallest addressable unit on a disk's track.

seek time   The actual amount of time it takes for a CD-ROM driver to move from reading one location to another.

SEGA CD   CD peripheral for a 16-bit Genesis system.

serial port   Standard port on the back of the computer for attaching peripheral devices. Data is sent in a single file.

server   A large computer that controls a network and allows shared access to resources.

SGML   Standard Graphics Markup Language.

shareware   Software available for trial from software groups and bulletin boards.

shielding   Protecting transmission hardware to prevent interference.

single session   A photo CD with only one set of images.

site license   A software license that allows unlimited copying of a computer program for use by a single organization at a specified location.

software   Specific instructions that computers use to perform specific tasks.

software driver   Hardware that helps a computer communicate directly with a peripheral device.

sound board   Hardware that helps IBM-compatible computers broadcast quality sound from digitized sources.

spin-up time   The time required for a CD-ROM at rest to get up to speed.

standalone   A self-contained CD-ROM player external to the computer.

standards   Rules for software production, format, or access.

star   A LAN topology where all network nodes are directly connected to a central hub.

STP   Shielded Twisted-Pair cable.

sub directory   A disk directory that is stored within another directory.

surge protector   A device used to protect equipment against sudden electrical surges.

SVGA   Super VGA. Improved VGA resolution and increased number of colors for IBM compatibles.

telecopy   Fax.

terminal   A computer output device where a user receives information, i.e., monitor or screen.

text   Character strings usually stored and transmitted in ASCII.

thesaurus   A list of designated words or descriptors to help when searching a database.

TIFF   A graphics file format.

token ring   A LAN topology where data is only transmitted when a flag or token is present.

topology   The physical and logical characteristics of a LAN such as star, ring, or bus.

tower   A hardware peripheral with internal CD-ROM drives.

track   A continuous CD segment.

transceiver   Interface device in Ethernet installations.

transfer rate   Speed at which a CD-ROM player displays information on a screen.

TSR   Terminate and Stay Resident. Software that loads into memory before other software can be executed.

turnkey system   A complete system bought from one vendor that contains everything needed to start working.

tutorial   A form of instruction where the student is guided step by step through the application of a program to a specific task.

twisted-pair   Cable with two wires twisted through their entire length.

Ultimedia   IBM's standard for multimedia. Runs on a PS/2 computer and supports CD-ROM XA and DVI.

UNIX   Operating system developed by Bell Labs.

update   Bring a database up-to-date by adding new information or a new version of a software package.

upload   To transfer data from a local computer to another computer.

utilities   Programs that assist in the operations of a computer but do not do the main work.

VGA   Video Graphics Array. Monitor used by IBM-compatibles for multimedia applications.

VHS   Video Home System. Standard consumer videotape.

video capture   see **frame grabber**.

videodisc   An optically encoded disc containing up to 54,000 analog images or 30 minutes of video.

virtual reality   A computer generated world where the user interacts with objects and initiates actions.

VIS Video Information System. A CD-ROM system from Tandy that connects to a television.

window A defined area on a screen which contains specific information.

Windows A graphical interface for IBM-compatible computers.

workgroup People with similar work-related needs who share resources.

workstation An individual computer or station on a LAN.

WORM Write Once Read Many. An optical system used to create a custom database where data is written once to a disk but can be read many times.

write To record data in computer storage.

write protect To prevent a floppy disk from accidentally being written over.

XGA Extended Graphics Adapter. Graphics standard that includes VGA.

Yellow Book Common name for standards developed for CD-ROM.

Search Tools/Internet Sites

List of Sites

http://cuiwww.unige.ch/w3catalog. CU1 W3 catalog. Interface to several manually maintained Internet catalogs.

http://ds.internic.net/ InterNIC Directory & Database Services. Very large searchable databases of Internet resources, provided by AT&T, General Atomics and Network Solutions.

http://gnn.com The Global Network Navigator (GNN) O'Reilly and Associates' access to the Whole Internet Catalog, an online marketplace, and several special-interest newsletters.

http://harvest.cs.colorado.edu The Harvest Information Discovery and Access System. Lets you build brokers that assist with Internet searches.

http://lib-www.ucr.edu/govpub/ Infomine. Good selection of links to government sites.

http://lycos.cs.cmu.edu Lycos. Carnegie-Mellon University's Internet search tool. Very highly regarded, but massive and often overloaded.

http://sunsite.unc.edu/boutell/faq/www_faq.htlm WWW Frequently Asked Questions. Basic questions and answers about the Web, updated frequently.

http://town.hall.org/ Internet Town Hall. A good starting position from which to locate resources all over the Web.

http://web.nexor.co.uk/public/welcome.html Nexor Public Services. Powerful key-word searches for Web resources.

http://webcrawler.com WebCrawler. Contains 350,000 Web documents indexed for keyword searching. Fast and comprehensive.

http://www.clas.ufl.edu/CLAS/american-universities.html List of American universities. A list of more than 150 college and university Web home pages.

http://www.cs.colorado.edu/home/mcbryan/WWWW.html World Wide Web Worm. An automated search system that scans the Web for you, then creates a personal, searchable catalog.

http://www.cs.colorado.edu/-mcbryan/bb/summary.html Mother-of-all-BBS. A subject-oriented index of Web pages.

http://www.directory.net Open Market's Commercial Sites Index. A list of more than 2,500 links to commercial, government and nonprofit home pages.

http://www.einet.net/galaxy.html EINet Galaxy. Very complete catalog of Internet resources.

http://www.lib.umich.edu/chhome.html   Clearinghouse for Internet Resource Guides.

http://www.netsurf.com/nsd/index.html   Netsurfer Digest. A free weekly magazine about the Web. Must subscribe, must choose either straight text or text with hyperlinks. Subscribers also get a weekly, promotional mailing.

http://www.stir.ac.uk/jsbin/js   JumpStation. Uses "robots" to compile Web indexes by subject, title and document header. Uneven results.

http://www.uwm.edu/Mirror/inet.services.html   Formerly the University of North Carolina Heliocentric Information Map, noted for its circular menus with UNC at the center of the information universe. Now serves as homepage for Internet Services List by Scott Yanoff (the "Yanoff List"). The University of North Carolina heliocentric information map may now be found at **http://sunsite.unc.edu/heliocentric.html.**

http://www.w3.org/hypertext/DataSources/bySubject/Overview.html   The WWW Virtual Library. Includes subject and geographical indexes to Web pages.

http://www.yahoo.com/   Yahoo. Massive index to Web pages organized by category. Includes a search tool. Popular and crowded.

http://www.yellow.com   World Wide Yellow Pages. Lists all the businesses on the Web, with daily updates and links to searching tools.

Computing

http://index.almaden.ibm.com/   David Singer's OS/2 Page of Pointers. For OS/2 operating system users looking for the latest information.

http://www.apple.com   Apple Computer Inc. Product listings and support policies, technical white papers and research documents.

http://www.austin.ibm.com/pspinfo/   IBM Personal Software Co. Covers software, including latest OS/2 developments.

http://www.compaq.com/   Compaq Computer Corp. One of the best-looking Web sites. Product information and up-to-date device drivers.

http://www.digital.com   Digital Equipment Corp. Information about DEC's products, in easily searchable form.

http://www.hp.com   Hewlett-Packard Co. Access HP is a one-stop directory of all HP products.

http://www.ibm.com   IBM's main home page, with links to IBM locations worldwide, and to Advantis, IBM's Internet provider.

http://www.informix.com   Informix Software. InformixLink's main Web page with links to comprehensive information on this database vendor.

http://www.intel.com   Intel Corp. All aspects of Intel activities and products, beginning with an amusing opening screen.

http://www.lotus.com/   A test site for InterNotes Web Server, which connects Lotus Notes to the Web. Cutting-edge technology on display.

http://www.mcom.com   Netscape Communications Corp. Home page of *Netscape*, the most popular Web browser, with many interesting links.

http://www.microsoft.com   Microsoft Corp. Everything about Microsoft and its products, including the latest on *Windows 95*.

http://www.ncsa.uiuc.edu/General/NCSAHome.html   Web site for developers of *Mosaic*, the first widely used Web browser. Good late-breaking Web news.

http://www.nec.com/   NEC Corp. NEC product information in both English and Japanese.

http://www.netcom.com   Netcom On-Line Communication Services. Manufacturer of the *NetCruiser* Web browser. Lots of diverse Web links.

http://www.novell.com   Novell Inc. Information about the company's products, owners of WordPerfect.

http://www.oracle.com   Oracle Corp. Company and product information and white papers.

http://www.psi.net   Performance Systems International Inc. Home page of the largest Internet services provider; explains what PSI does and how.

http://www.sgi.com   Silicon Graphics Inc. Home page for enterprises famous for graphics products. Great screens that download slowly; a text-only version also available.

http://www.sun.com   Sun Microsystems Inc. Product information, and links to SunSites, Sun-sponsored Web servers at several universities.

http://www.sybase.com   Sybase Inc. Information about Sybase and connection to *Sybase SQL Server* on the Web.

http://www.taligent.com   Complex information about the company's products presented in a pleasant and accessible way.

http://www.us.dell.com   Dell Computer Corp. Latest pricing on Dell's Dimension computers.

http://www.w3.org/   CERN. The original Web home page, good for keeping up to date on Web matters.

http://www.ziff.com   Ziff-Davis Publishing. Access to *PC Magazine* and eight other computer publications.

Education/Fun/Fringe Activities

http://gertrude.art.uiuc.edu/@art/gallery.html   @art. A virtual art gallery sponsored by the University of Illinois.

http://sunsite.ucs.edu/cisco/cisco-home.html   The Cisco Educational Archive. Home page with links interesting to K–12 students and teachers.

http://town.hall.org/places/city_lights/   City Lights Publishers and Booksellers. San Francisco's best-known *avant garde* bookstore.

http://tns-www.lcs.mit.edu/cgi-bin/sports   World Wide Web of Sports. Complete sports home page, with links to sites in all sports.

http://wcl-rs.bham.ac.uk/GamesDomain   Games Domain. One-stop information about computer games and Internet online role-playing games.

http://www.city.net/   City.Net. Guides to several American cities, varying in depth and quality.

http://www.crc.ricoh.com/people/steve/kids.html   Interesting Places for Kids. Hundreds of links interesting to school-age children.

http://www.hotwired.com   *HotWired*. Online version of *Wired* magazine. You must sign up, but the subscription is free.

http://www.npac.syr.edu/textbook/kidsweb/math.html   Kid's Web — Math. This index of K–12 mathematic sites features geometry, puzzles, fractions, and educational games.

http://www.phantom.com/~giant/hype.html   *Hype ElectraZine.* Very interesting online electronic magazine, dazzling, entertaining; many links.

Government

http://lcweb.loc.gov/homepage/lchp.html   Library of Congress. Online exhibitions, tour of countries, etc.

http://thomas.loc.gov   Thomas Legislative Information on the Internet. Keyword-searchable store of all legislation from the last two sessions of Congress.

http://www.census.gov   U.S. Bureau of the Census. Much demographic information, but said to be hard to access.

http://www.epa.gov/   Environmental Production Agency. Searchable information about environmental matters.

http://www.fbi.gov   Federal Bureau of Investigation. Assorted items, including the 10-most-wanted list.

http://www.fedworld.gov   FedWorld Information Network. National Technical Information Center site, with information searching and ordering, links to other federal sites, and searchable government report abstracts.

http://www.fie.com/www/us_gov.htm   Federal Information Exchange List of WWW Servers (U.S. Government). Universal list of U.S. government locations, with hundreds of links to government agency sites. {".htm" may be a typo; ".html" is the normal address segment]

http://www.gsfc.nasa.gov/   National Aeronautics and Space Administration. General NASA information, news, tours of NASA installations.

http://www.house.gov   U.S. House of Representatives. Schedule of House activities, access to connected members, additional Capitol Hill information.

http://www.law.cornell.edu/constitution/constitution.overview.html   U.S. Constitution. The classic document presented in html format.

http://www.ncts.navy.mil/   U.S. Navy OnLine. "…is interesting more because it exists at all and is really well done than because of its content." [The same can be said about a lot of home pages!]

http://www.npr.gov   National Performance Review. Site for documents from the Vice President's project to reduce the size and increase the efficiency of the federal government.

http://www.odci.gov/   Central Intelligence Agency. CIA home page, with international affairs information.

http://www.whitehouse.gov   The White House. Assorted White House information, tours, quotes from Socks, pictures, historical information, current statistics on government agencies and consumerism, and the opportunity to sign the guest book.

Business/Commerce/Shopping

http://ananse.irv.uit.no/law/nav/law_ref.html   International links for trade information, links to the United Nations.

http://branch.com   Branch Mall. Branch Information Services' prototype online shopping mall, said not to be well stocked.

http://plaza.xor.com   The Internet Plaza. Shopping and some online ordering; many links still under construction.

http://sashimi.wwa.com/~notime/eotw/EOTW.html   Entrepreneurs on the Web. Site for small business and beginning entrepreneurs.

http://www.commerce.net   CommerceNet. Information about how to do business on the Internet, with links to a wide variety of business-related sites.

http://www.digicash.com/ecash/ecash-home.html   Ecash. Information about benefits and drawbacks of electronic cash for use online.

http://www.law.cornell.edu/   The Legal Information Institute. Information about business and the law.

http://www.quote.com   Quotecom. Stock prices, all kinds of international business information.

http://www.tig.com/IBC/   Internet Business Center. Information helpful to people contemplating doing business on the Internet.

http://www.uspto.gov/   U.S. Patent and Trademark Office. Information about copyrights and patents.

Library Reference Web Sites

http://biomed.nus.sg/vh/vh.html   Web Server for the Visually Handicapped.

http://deafworldweb.org/deafworld/   Deafworld Web.

http://ericpsed.uiuc.edu/nccic/nccichome.html   National Child Care Information Center.

http://kidshealth.org/   Kidshealth.

http://www.albany.net/allinone   The All-in-One Search Page.

http://www.cyberkids.com   Cyberkids.

http://www.ed.gov/   U.S. Dept. of Education.

http://www.inform.umd.edu:8080/EdRes/ReadingRoom   The Reading Room provides access to online books, poetry, journals and other topics relating to reading.

http://www.iquest.net/greatconnect/oneaddplace/1   Attention Deficit Disorders.

http://www.lib.usm.edu/degrumm.htm   Children's Literature Web Guides.

http://www.loc.gov/   Library of Congress World Wide Web.

http://www.nas.com/downsyn/information.html   Down Syndrome.

http://www.netrus.net/users/peace/govt_em.htm   U.S. Government Addresses.

http://www.nim.nth.gov/   National Library of Medicine.

http://www.slip.net/~scmetro/childeo.htm   Youth & Children Resources Net.

Science and Technology

http://seds.lpl.arizona edu/nineplanets/nineplanets.html   The Nine Planets. This
multimedia Tour of the Solar System features each of the planets and major
moons with illustrated photographs from NASA. Background information is
presented about each planet.

http://sgisrvr.asc.edu/index.html   SuperComputing. The Alabama Supercomputer Authority is a state-funded corporation founded in 1989 to operate the
Alabama Supercomputer Center and the Alabama Research and Education Network. The mission is to provide supercomputing time and related resources to
Alabama's academic researchers and industry. The network AREN, provides
internet connectivity to state government, industry, higher education and K–12
systems within the State of Alabama.

http://sunsite.unc.edu   University of North Carolina–Chapel Hill. The goals of the
SunSite (Software, Information and Technology Exchange) are to: provide easy
access to public domain software on the internet; act as a repository for Sun and
key government information; promote development and research of new internet tools; and launch cutting-edge applications on the internet. Since 1992,
SunSite has expanded to several key universities around the world.

http://www.arlut.utexas.edu   University of Texas–ARLUT. Applied Research Lab-
oratories, located at the University of Texas at Austin, provides access to many
divisions within ARL.UT WWW services including CSD (Computer Science
Division), SGG (Space and Geophysics Group, ITG (Information Technology
Group), NAD (Nonlinear Acoustics Division), ASD (Advanced Sonar Division) and APL-Personnel Office. Navigational Resources for general searches are
Lycos, Alta Vista, Infoseek, WebCrawler, the Internet Sleuth, CUI World Wide
Web Catalog, World Map, the WWW Virtual Library, the Yahoo Web Database and People Helping One Another Know Stuff (PHOAKS). Many other services are available, including Educational Resources, Technical Resources, Computer Software and Hardware Resources, University of Texas at Austin, Local
and National Weather Information, and Local and Miscellaneous Resources.

http://www.cs.indiana.edu   Technical Reports Archive. The Indiana University
Bloomington Computer Science Department provides WWW Services to
Unified Computer Science Technical Report Index, ALIWEB mirror, Finger
gateway with faces, Picons Archive/Search, Local Weather, Noetica e-journal
mirror, and the Types Forum. Available Access to Groups, Labs, and Projects
are Analog VLSI and Robotics Lab, Artificial Intelligence Lab, Computer Systems Group, Database Group, Graphics Lab, Hardware Methods Group, Programming Languages Group, Scientific Computing Group, Visual Inference
Lab and Scheme educational-infrastructure project. Other groups, labs, and
projects may be added.

http://www.hpcc.gov   National Coordination Office for Computing, Information,
and Communications. The NCO provides a central point of CCIC (Committee on Computing, Information, and Communications) contact to the U.S.
Congress, federal agencies, state and local organizations, foreign organizations,
academia, industry, and the public. The NCO supports the National Science
and Technology Council. The web site provides access to the NCO for CIC,

HPCC Publications, Federal Networking Council, Applications Council, Grants and Awards, the White House, Legislation and Testimony, Agency and Activity Servers, What's New, and Links to Related Information.

http://www.tc.cornell.edu Cornell Theory Center Overview. The Cornell Theory Center is one of four high performance computing and communications centers supported by the National Science Foundation. Activities of the center are also funded by New York State, the Advanced Research Projects Agency, the National Center for Research Resources at the National Institutes of Health, IBM, and other members of CTC's Corporate Partnership Program. A variety of education and training programs are offered to high school, undergraduate, and graduate students, and their teachers. Cornell Theory Center's reputation as an international resource is based on its: interdisciplinary research collaborations among academia, industry, and government researchers; integrated and highly parallel high-performance computing environment; world-class education and training programs; Powerful local, national, and international technology exchange networks.

Bibliography

Access Faxon. Westbrook, MA: Faxon Press, 1989.

ACCESS PENNSYLVANIA: An Agenda for Knowledge and Information Through Libraries. Harrisburg, PA: State Library of Pennsylvania, 1984.

Ackerman, Katherine. "Looking It Up in the Online Encyclopedias." *Link-Up* 3 (June 1986): 21–22.

AIIM Buying Guide: The Official Registry of Information and Image Management Products and Services. Silver Springs, MD: AIIM, 1985.

Alberico, Ralph. *Microcomputers for the Online Searcher.* Westport, CT: Meckler Publishing, 1987.

Ambron, Sueann, and Kristina Hooper, eds. *Interactive Micromedia.* Redmond, WA: Microsoft, 1988.

Arms, Caroline. "Using the National Networks: BITNET and the Internet." *Online* (September 1990): 24–29.

Armstrong, C.J., and J.A. Large. *CD-ROM Information Products: An Evaluative Guide and Directory.* Brookfield, VT: Gower Publishing, 1990.

Association of American Universities/Association of Research Libraries. *Reports of the AAU Task Force.* Washington, DC: Association of Research Libraries, 1994.

Aversa, Elizabeth Smith, and Jacqueline C. Mancall. *Management of Online Search Services in Schools.* Santa Barbara, CA: ABS-CLIO, 1989.

_____, _____, and Diane Oesau. *Online Information Services for Secondary School Students: A Current Assessment.* Syracuse, NY: ERIC Clearinghouse on Information Resources, 1988.

Babits, Ann. *CD-ROM Librarian Index: 1986–1990.* Westport, CT: Meckler Publishing, 1991.

Bailey, Charles W. "Electronic (Online) Publishing in Action … The Public-Access Computer Systems Review and Other Electronic Serials." *Online* (January 1991): 25–28.

Balas, Janet. "Searching CompuServe, Genie, and the Source." *Small Computers in Libraries* 7 (November 1987): 28–36.

Batt, Fred. *Online Searching for End Users: An Information Sourcebook.* Phoenix, AZ: Oryx, 1988.

Beiser, Karl. "Optical Product Review: Microsoft Bookshelf." *CD-ROM Librarian* 2 (November/December 1987): 27–34.

Bohl, Janet. "Optical Product Review: McGraw-Hill's CD-ROM Science and Technical Reference Set." *CD-ROM Librarian* 3 (February 1988): 29–32.

Brandt, Richard. *Videodisc Training: A Cost Analysis.* VA: Videodisc Monitor, 1989.

Brunell, David H. "Comparing CD-ROM Products." *CD-ROM Librarian* 3 (March 1988): 14–18.

Byerly, Greg. *Online and On-disc Searching: A Dictionary and Bibliographic Guide.* 3rd ed. Englewood, CO: Libraries Unlimited, 1988.

Callison, Daniel. "School Library Media Programs and Free Inquiry Learning." *School Library Journal* 32:6 (1986): 20–24.

Caputo, Anne S. "DIALOG in the School: Use of DIALOG's Classroom Instruction Program in Secondary Schools." *Education Libraries* 11 (Winter 1986): 5–7.

The CD-ROM Directory. England: TFPL Publishing, 1989.

CD-ROM Market Place, 1991: An International Directory. Westport, CT: Meckler Publishing, 1991.

CD-ROM Yearbook. Bellevue, WA: Microsoft Press, 1989.

CD-ROMs in Print. Westport, CT: Meckler Publishing, 1989.

Chen, Ching-chih, and Susanna Schweizer. *Online Bibliographic Searching: A Learning Manual.* New York, NY: Neal-Schuman Publishers, Inc., 1981.

Chesley, Harry R. "A Hypercard Front-End to DIALOG." *Apple Library Users Group Newsletter* 5 (October 1987): 50–51.

Compact Optical Disc Technology — CD-ROM, April 1979–1986: Citations from the INSPEC Database. Springfield, VA: National Technical Information Service, 1986.

Consortium of College and University Media Centers/Agency for Instructional Technology. *Educational Fair Access and the New Media National Conference.* Washington, DC: CCUMC/AIT, 1994.

Costa, Betty, and Marie Costa. *A Micro Handbook for Small Libraries and Media Centers.* 2nd ed. Littleton, CO: Libraries Unlimited, 1986.

Costigan, Dan. *Laser-Optical Storage: The New Dimension in Information Automation.* Bethesda, MD: Avedon Associates, 1988.

Csaszar, Imre. "Linking Components in the Electronic Meeting Room." *Presentation Products Magazine* (February 1990): 65.

A Curriculum Guide for Online Database Searching with High School Students. Ankeny, IA: Heartland Education Agency, 1985.

Davies, Ruth A. *The School Library Media Program: Instructional Force for Excellence.* 3rd ed. New York: Bowker, 1979.

DeLoughry, T. "Administration Panel Uses High-Tech Razzle-Dazzle to Illustrate Promise of the Information Superhighway." *The Chronicle of Higher Education* (September 14, 1994): A50.

_____. "Effort to Provide Scholarly Journals by Computer Tries to Retain the Look and Feel of Printed Publications." *The Chronicle of Higher Education* (April 7, 1993): A19–20.

_____. "State-of-the-art Moot Courtroom Unveiled at William and Mary." *The Chronicle of Higher Education* (September 22, 1993): A22–23.

Desmarais, Norman, ed. *CD-ROM Local Area Networks: A User's Guide.* Westport, CT: Meckler Publishing, 1991.

_____, ed. *CD-ROM Reviews, 1987–1990: Optical Product Reviews from CD-ROM Librarian.* Westport, CT: Meckler Publishing, 1991.

_____, ed. *CD-ROMs in Print, 1992.* Westport, CT: Meckler Publishing, 1991.

_____, ed. *The Librarians's CD-ROM Handbook.* Westport, CT: Meckler Publishing, 1989.

Directory of Online Databases 9:1 (January 1988). New York: Cuadra/Elsevier, 1988.

Ditlea, Steve. "HyperTed." *PC/Computing* (October 1990): 201–210.

Drummond, Louis. "Going Beyond Online." *Online* (September 1990): 6–8.

Duggan, Mary K. *CD-ROM in the Library: Today and Tomorrow.* New York: G.K. Hall, 1990.

_____. "Copyright of Electronic Information: Issues and Questions." *Online* (May 1991): 20–26.

Dunman, Susan. "ERIC: An Essential Online Tool for Educators." *Electronic Learning* 7 (January 1988): 45.

Educational Videodisc Directory. Washington, DC: Systems Impact, 1989.

EDUCOM. "The Bill of Rights and Responsibilities for Electronic Learners." *EDUCOM Review* 28:3 (1993).

"EINSTEIN: A Solution to Online Searching in Schools?" *School Library Media Activities Monthly* 4 (October 1987): 45, 50.

Eisenberg, Michael and Robert E. Berdowitz. *Curriculum Initiative: An Agenda and Strategy for Library Media Programs.* Norwood, NJ: Ablex, 1988.

Eisenberg, Michael Brown. "Current Themes Regarding Library and Information Skills Instruction: Research Supporting and Research Lacking." *School Library Media Quarterly* (1992): 102–108.

Elmore, Garland. "Planning and Developing a Multimedia Learning Environment." *T.H.E. Journal* (February 1991): 83–88.

Elshami, Ahmed M. *CD-ROM Technology for Information Managers.* Chicago, IL: American Library Association, 1990.

Emard, Jean-Paul, ed. *CD-ROMs in Print 1988–1989.* Westport, CT: Meckler Publishing, 1988.

Engle, Mary. "Summary of PACS-L Readers Response Concerning Designing Systems to Support Reading Electronic Books." BITNET communication, February 12, 1991.

Ensor, Pat. *CD-ROM Research Collections.* Westport, CT: Meckler Publishing, 1991.

_____, and Steve Hardin. *CD-ROM Periodical Index.* Westport, CT: Meckler Publishing, 1991.

Epler, Doris M. *Online Searching Goes to School.* Phoenix, AZ: Oryx, 1989.

Fayen, Emily Gallup. "The Answer Machine and Direct Connect: Do-It-Yourself Searching in Libraries." *Online* 12 (September 1988): 13–21.

Feldman, Tony. *The Publisher's Guide to CD-ROM.* New York: Van Nostrand Reinhold, 1991.

Fenichel, Carol H. and Thomas H. Hogan. *Online Searching: A Primer.* 2nd ed. Medford, NJ: Learned Information, 1984.

Ferrarini, Elizabeth M. *INFOMANIA: The Guide to Essential Electronic Services.* Boston, MA: Houghton Mifflin Co., 1985.

Fink, Teri. "LaserCat Goes to High School." *Wilson Library Bulletin* 62 (March 1988): 55–56, 109.

Fissel, Charles. "The Video Information System: Is It 'Fest Educational Tool Around'?" *T.H.E. Journal* (December 1990): 59–61.

Fox, David. *The CD-ROM Market in Canadian Libraries.* Westport, CT: Meckler Publishing, 1990.

Fox, Jackie. "When Worlds Collide: Demystifying Multimedia." *PC Today* (June 1991): 6.

Franz, R.R. "Real Teaching in the Social Context of the Virtual School" in *Technology and Teacher Education Annual,* eds. B. Robin, J. Price, J. Willis, and D.A. Willis. Charlottesville, VA: Association for the Advancement of Computing in Education, 1996.

Freeman, Craig C., and Eileen K. Schofied. *Roadside Wildflowers of the Southern Great Plains.* Lawrence, KS: University of Kansas Press, 1991.

Gale, John. *State of the CD-ROM Industry: Applications, Players, and Products.* Alexandria, VA: Information Workstation Group, 1987.

____, Clifford Lynch, and Edward Brownrigg. *Report on CD-ROM Search Software.* Alexandria, VA: Information Workstation Group, 1987.

Garrett, John R. "Text to Screen Revisited: Copyright in the Electronic Age." *Online* (March 1991): 22–24.

Gerber, Carole Houze. "Einstein." *Media & Methods* 24 (November/December 1987): 42–43.

Glossbrenner, Alfred. *How to Look It Up Online.* New York, NY: St. Martin's Press, 1987.

Guide to Producing Videodiscs in NTSC and PAL. Dover, DE: Philips and DuPont Optical Company, 1989.

Hall, James L., and Marjorie J. Brown, eds. *Online Bibliographic Databases: An International Directory.* 4th ed. Detroit, MI: Gale Research, 1986.

Hane, Paula. "Paper: The Security Blanket of the Electronic Age." *Database* (February 1991): 6–7.

Hart, Michael. "Information About Project Gutenberg." BITNET communication, May 11, 1990.

____. "Project Gutenberg: Access to Electronic Texts." *Database* (December 1990): 6–9.

Harter, Stephen P. *Online Information Retrieval: Concepts, Principles, and Techniques.* Orlando, FL: Academic Press, Inc., 1986.

Hartley, R.J., et al. *Online Searching: Principles and Practice.* 2nd ed. Stoneham, MA: Butterworth, 1988.

Heid, Jim. "Getting Started with HyperCard." *MacWorld* (May 1989): 243–253.

Helgerson, Linda. *CD-ROM: Electronic Publishing in Business and Industry.* New York: Van Nostrand Reinhold, 1991.

____. "Optical Disc Technology." *T.H.E. Journal* (June 1987): 46–51.

____, and Martin Ennis. *The CD-ROM Sourcedisc.* Alexandria, VA: Diversified Data Resources, Inc., 1987.

Hendley, Tony. *CD-ROM and Optical Publishing Systems.* Westport, CT: Meckler Publishing, 1987.

Hollander, Robert. "Brief Description of Project." BITNET communication, February 21, 1991.

Holloway, Carson. "Books in Print and Ulrich's on CD-ROM: A Preliminary Review." *Online* 11 (September 1987): 57–61.

Honey, M. and A. Henriquez. *Telecommunications and K-12 Educators: Findings from a National Survey.* New York: Bank Street College of Education, 1993.

Horne, Dorice. "A Look at Wilsearch." *Small Computers in Libraries* 7 (December 1987): 29–34.

Hunter, Beverly, and Erica K. Lodish. *Online Searching in the Curriculum.* Santa Barbara, CA: ABC-CLIO, 1988.

INFOhio 2000: Information Programs for the 21st Century. Columbus, OH: Ohio Educational Library/Media Association and Ohio Department of Education, 1992.

Information and Image Management: The State of the Industry 1989. Silver Spring, MD: AIIM, 1989.

Information Power: Guidelines for School Library Media Programs. Chicago, IL: American Association of School Librarians and Association for Educational Communications Technology, 1988.

Information Skills Curriculum Guide. Olympia, WA: Washington Library Media Association, 1989.

Information 2000: Library and Information Services for the 21st Century, from the *Final Report of the 1991 White House Conference on Library and Information Services.* U.S. National Commission on Libraries and Information Science, 1992.

Integrating Information-Management Skills: A Process for Incorporating Library Media Skills Into Content Areas. Harrisonburg, PA: Department of Education, Division of School Library Media Services, 1988.

Interactive Videodiscs for Education. Lexington, KY: Ztek Co., 1989.

Irving, Ann. *Study and Information Skills Across the Curriculum.* Portsmouth, NH: Heinemann, 1985.

Isailovic, Jordan. *Videodisc Systems: Theory and Applications.* Englewood Cliffs, NJ: Prentice Hall, 1987.

Johnsen, Anne M. "A Review of Databases for Education." *Education Libraries* 9 (Spring 1984): 5–9.

Karraker, Roger. "Crisis in American Education: Can Multimedia Save the Day?" *New Media* (January 1992).

Kellner, Mark. "Multimedia's Mounting Momentum." *InfoWorld* (October 21, 1991): 58.

Kent, Frances, and Julie Price. "Wilsonline Helps High School Students Develop Research and Writing Skills." *School Library Media Quarterly* 16 (Winter 1988): 135.

King, James. "The Lesson of Cooperative Learning Is a Lesson for Life." *Media Spectrum* (Summer 1991): 20–22.

Kinnaman, Daniel E. "The Problem with Information in the Information Age." *Technology and Learning* 15:1 (September 1994): 94.

Kleiner, Jane P. "InfoTrac: An Evaluation of System Use and Potential in Research Libraries." *RQ* 27 (Winter 1987): 252–263.

Kovacs, David. *The Internet Training Guide.* New York: Van Nostrand Reinhold, 1995.

Krapp, J.V. "An Emerging Theory of Library Instruction." *School Library Media Quarterly* 16:1 (1988): 23–28.

Krimmelbein, Cindy Jeffrey. *The Choice to Change: Establishing an Integrated School Library Media Program.* Littleton, CO: Libraries Unlimited, 1989.

Kuhlthau, Carol C. "Information Search Process: A Summary of Research and

Implications for School Library Media Programs." *School Library Media Quarterly* (1989): 19–25.

_____. "A Process Approach to Library Skills Instruction." *School Library Media Quarterly* 13 (1985): 35–40.

Lachner, Lewis Eric. "Documented Success." *Beyond Computing,* April 1996.

Lambert, Steve, and Suzanne Ropiequet, eds. *The New Papyrus, CD-ROM.* Bellevue, WA: Microsoft Press, 1986.

Lee, Joann H. *Online Searching: The Basics, Settings, and Management.* 2nd ed. Englewood, CO: Libraries Unlimited, 1989.

Li, Xia, and Nancy B. Crane. *Electronic Style: A Guide to Citing Electronic Information.* Westport, CT: Meckler Publishing, 1993.

Lit, Tze-chung. *An Introduction to Online Searching.* Westport, CT: Greenwood Press, 1985.

Loertscher, David. *Taxonomies of the School Library Media Program.* Littleton, CO: Libraries Unlimited, 1988.

McQueen, Judy, and Richard W. Boss. *Videodisc and Optical Digital Disk Technologies and Their Applications in Libraries.* Chicago, IL: American Library Association, 1986.

Magel, Mark. "The Many Faces of Multimedia." *AV Video* (September 1990): 68.

Maloney, James J., ed. *Online Searching Technique and Management.* Chicago, IL: American Library Association, 1983.

Mancall, Jacqueline C., and Carl M. Drott. *Measuring Student Information Use: A Guide for School Library Media Specialists.* Littleton, CO: Libraries Unlimited, 1983.

_____, Erica K. Lodish, and Judith Springer. "Searching Across the Curriculum." *Phi Delta Kappan* 73:7 (1992): 526–532.

Maracaccio, Kathleen Young. *Computer-Readable Databases: A Directory and Data Sourcebook.* Detroit, MI: Gale Research, 1989.

Martin, William. "Touring an Informational Wonderland." *Classroom Computer Learning* 4 (February 1984): 52, 57–58, 60.

Micrographic and Optical Recording Buyers Guide. England: Spectrum Publishing, 1989.

Mills, Steven C. "Integrated Learning Systems." *Tech Trends* 39:1 (January/February 1994): 27–28.

Montgomery, Paula Kay. "Integrating Library, Media, Research, and Information Skills." *Phi Delta Kappan* 73:7 (1992): 529–532.

Montgomery County Public Schools. *Instructional Objectives for Information Retrieval and Media Production.* Rockville, MD: Montgomery County Public Schools, 1978.

Morabito, Margaret. "Education by Modem: A Selection of Services." *Link-Up* 4 (April 1987): 14–15.

Morrow, Blaine. "WILSONDISC's Readers' Guide Abstracts." *CD-ROM Librarian* 3 (October 1988): 21–27.

Morton, Bruce. "Computer-Based Information: Online and on Disc." *Library Hi Tech News,* no. 36 (March 1987): 1, 8–9.

Nelson, Nancy Melin. *Library Application of Optical Disk and CD-ROM Technology.* Westport, CT: Meckler Publishing, 1987.

_____, and Meta Nissley. *CD-ROM Licensing and Copyright Issues for Libraries*. Westport, CT: Meckler Publishing, 1990.

Nicholls, Paul. *CD-ROM Collection Builder's Toolkit*. Weston, CT: Pemberton Press, 1990.

1988 Medicaldisc Directory. Alexandria, VA: Paul R. Stewart Publishing, 1988.

Oberg, Antoinette. "The School Librarian and the Classroom Teacher: Partners in Curriculum Planning." *Emergency Librarian* 14 (1986): 9–14.

O'Leary, Mick. "Easy Net Revisited: Pushing the Online Frontier." *Online* 12 (September 1988): 22–30.

_____. "Magazine Index: The People's Choice." *Link-Up* 4 (September/October 1987): 12, 25.

"Online." *The Chronicle of Higher Education*. (September 22, 1994): 23.

Optical Memory Data Storage , 1975–February 1986: Citations from the INSPEC Database. Springfield, VA: National Technical Information Service, 1986.

Optical Storage Technology 1987: A State of the Art Review. Westport, CT: Meckler Publishing, 1987.

Palmer, Roger C. *Online Reference and Information Retrieval*. 2nd ed. Littleton, CO: Libraries Unlimited, Inc., 1987.

Parisi, Lynn S. and Virginia L. Jones. *Directory of Online Databases and CD-ROM Resources for High Schools*. Santa Barbara, CA: ABC-CLIO, 1988.

Pennsylvania Online: A Curriculum Guide for School Library Media Centers. State Department of Education, 1990.

Pruitt, Ellen, and Diane Walker-Allison. *Library Media Center Resource Pathfinders*. Rockville, MD: Montgomery County Public Schools, 1986.

Publication Manual of the American Psychological Association — 4th edition. Washington, DC: American Psychological Association, 1994.

Purcell, Royal. "Electronic ERIC." *Small Computers in Libraries* 8 (February 1988): 18–21.

_____. "Laser Videodisc Stores Periodicals Indexing." *Small Computers in Libraries* 7 (April 1987): 19–22.

Rankin, Virginia. "Pre-Search: Intellectual Access to Information." *School Library Journal* (March 1992): 168–170.

_____. "Rx: Task Analysis or, Relief for the Major Discomforts of Research Assignments." *School Library Journal* (November 1992): 29–32.

Rechel, Michael W. "Laser Disc Technology: A Selective Introductory Bibliography." *CD-ROM Librarian* 2 (4) (July/August 1987): 16–24.

Reese, Jean, and Ramona Steffey. "ERIC on CD-ROM: A Comparison of Dialog OnDisc, OCLC's Search CD450 and SilverPlatter." *Online* 11 (September 1987): 42–54.

Research Goes to School II: How to Go Online to the Databases. Olympia, WA: Washington Superintendent of Public Instruction, 1985.

Ropiequet, Suzanne, ed. *CD-ROM 2: Optical Publishing*. Bellevue, WA: Microsoft Press, 1987.

Roth, Judith Paris. *Essential Guide to CD-ROM*. Westport, CT: Meckler, 1986.

Ryan, Joe. "CD-ROM Databases: A Sampling." *CD-ROM Librarian* 3 (September 1988): 28–29.

Saffady, William. *Optical Disks for Data and Document Storage*. Westport, CT: Meckler Publishing, 1986.

Schneebeck, C. "Copyright Law: Providing Access to Information." *Educational Fair Access and the New Media National Conference.* Washington, DC: CCUMC/AIT, 1994.

Schultz, Elizabeth. "A New Face Everyday." *Teacher Magazine* (November/December 1991).

Serra, Dan. "Newspaper Databases for Locating Articles." *Link-Up* 4 (February 1987): 20.

Sherman, Chris, ed. *The CD-ROM Handbook.* New York, NY: McGraw Hill, 1988.

Smith, Karen E. "Hypertext-Linking to the Future." *Online* 12 (March 1988): 32–40.

Steele, Ken. "Shakespeare Electronic Conference Update." BITNET communication, November 21, 1990.

Stripling, Barbara K. and Judy M. Pitts. *Brainstorms and Blueprints: Teaching Library Research as a Thinking Process.* Littleton, CO: Libraries Unlimited, 1988.

Suggested Learner Outcomes. Oklahoma City: State Department of Education, 1987.

Tenopir, Carol. "General Literature Online: Magazine Index & Readers' Guide." *Library Journal* 11 (May 1, 1986): 92–93.

____. *Issues on Online Database Searching.* Englewood, CO: Libraries Unlimited, 1989.

Timbers, Jill G. "Laserdisc Technology: A Review of the Literature on Videodisc and Optical Disc Technology, 1983–mid-1985." *Library Hi Tech Bibliography 1* (1986): 57–66.

Ting, David, and Eric Winakur. *Montgomery County Public Schools DIALOG User's Manual, Introductory Level.* Rockville, MD: Montgomery County Public Schools, 1984.

Toor, Ruth and Hilda K. Weisburg. *Sharks, Ships, and Potato Chips: Curriculum Integrated Library Instruction.* Berkeley Heights, NJ: Library Learning Resources, Inc., 1986.

Troutner, Joanne. *The Media Specialist, the Microcomputer, and the Curriculum.* Edited by Shirley L. Aaron. Littleton, CO: Libraries Unlimited Inc., 1983.

Turner, Philip. *Helping Teachers Teach.* Littleton, CO: Libraries Unlimited, 1989.

Videodisc and Optical Digital Disk Technologies and Their Applications in Libraries. Washington, DC: Council on Library Resources.

Videodiscs, Compact Disks and Digital Optical Disk Systems. Medford, NJ: Learned Information, 1986.

Williams, Martha E., ed. *Annual Review of Information Science and Technology, Vol. 2.* White Plains, NY: Knowledge Industry Publications, Inc., 1986.

Willmott, Don. "The World Wide Web: A Guided Tour of 100 Hot Sites." *PC Magazine* 14:7 (1995): 37–42.

Wisconsin Library and Information Skills Guide. Madison, WI: Wisconsin Association of School Librarians, 1992.

Woolls, E. Blance, and David V. Loertscher, eds. *The Microcomputer Facility and the School Library Media Specialist.* Chicago, IL: American Library Association, 1986.

Index